DESIGN ORIGIN
SERIES

Design Origin:
France

First published and distributed by
viction:workshop ltd.

viction:ary™

viction:workshop ltd.
Unit C, 7/F, Seabright Plaza, 9-23 Shell Street,
North Point, Hong Kong
Url: www.victionary.com   Email: we@victionary.com
www.facebook.com/victionworkshop
www.twitter.com/victionary_
www.weibo.com/victionary

Edited and produced by viction:ary

Concepts & art direction by Victor Cheung
Book design by viction:workshop ltd.

ISBN 978-988-13204-4-5
Printed and bound in China

*Statistics on the book cover might not illustrate the reality in all aspects.

Design Origin : France

Graphics / Illustration / Art direction / Photography

DESIGN ORIGIN
SERIES

Designs in France Today.

"With the defining features and the historical wealth French graphics contain, we can keep on anticipating how the 'French attitude' would evolve through time."

———

Say What Studio

A creative approach denotes the process that combines the ends and the means to present an idea. In the context of this preface, the means refer to the format, material or techniques used, and the ends are specific to each case.

Although globalisation has evened out cultures and differences, each country has developed its own creative approach that conveys the past, its own heritage and its own culture. As when every culture has its own references and perception of the world, this leads to the formation of 'collective unconscious' within each society.

Historically, France has always been a country that holds arts and crafts in high regard. This emphasis on arts brings about a creative process strongly driven towards aesthetics and consequently special attention to the appearance of the end product. The fact that there are relatively less prestigious design schools in France, compared to her prominent neighbours such as Germany and Switzerland, does not stop French design from advancing. French design still stands out in many ways as designers would persistently improve their skills by acquiring new knowledge and skills about what they do.

What we mean by this is that, despite the fact that the French lack the prestigious training of schools like ECAL in Switzerland, the design they produce is pretty outstanding, perhaps for the same reason. They seek further education and training in the matter by constantly improving their skills.

From Belle Époque at the turn of the nineteenth century to the digital present, the French have always brought vitality and dynamism to the arts by paying particular attention to the presentation, its design and especially its execution. Today, French graphic design has evolved, but continues to convey these concepts with due care and attention. Some share a common interest in adornment with Japanese design, traditionally known for sober and minimalist aesthetics.

On the other hand, for historical reasons, countries like Germany and Switzerland project greater focus on industry and technology, which contributes to a decidedly more modern and practical approach. In these cultures, graphic designers keep on simplifying their expressions to achieve practical and logical purposes rather than a subjective one. This approach is more than just an influence, as it is now fully integrated into their culture, and forms part of their daily life.

Without going as back as the invention of typesetting and fonts, these differences in the creative attitude are highly represented and noticeable in certain artistic currents. As an illustration, we can draw a parallel between two contrasting design styles that emerged in Europe about the same time.

At the beginning of the twentieth century, France was embracing Art Nouveau. This then audacious style has been greatly embodied by French graphic designer George Auriol and his works, mixing illustration with complex geometric shapes. Simultaneously, Plakatstil emerged in Berlin in 1905, initiated by German graphic designer Lucian Bernhard. This style introduced catchy lettering, simplified shapes and characters to traditional advertising. One of this groundbreaking movement's most celebrated ambassadors was German poster artist Ludwig Hohlwein, who drew on the country's industrial background, and rendered more than 3,000 classic print ads for Audi, Bahlsen, BMW, Daimler Benz, Lufthansa, MAN, Pelikan and Henkel during his long career.

The Art Deco era followed, led by French and Ukrainian-French graphic artists Roland Ansieau and Cassandre. Their work translated bold geometric shapes into print advertisements. The ornamental movement strongly differed from the modern theories, styles, materials and design methods that were firmly advocated by German Bauhaus. The difference persisted during the 1950s, through the iconic typographic works of Max Miedinger (Helvetica) in Switzerland and Roger Excoffon (Banco and Mistral) in France. This approach remains today, visible in the works of Paris-based studio Les Graphiquants and those of Deutsche & Japaner in Manheim.

Over the past years, the Digital Shift has deeply shaken the foundations of the industry's creative approach. As the Internet and its channels continue to expand, references become more accessible and easily overshared and abused, quickly turning great ideas into vulgar ones. However, there also seems to be a new movement. Graphic design has become free of nationalities. Although there are fewer rules to comply with, there is a greater number of new design principles to follow, forming volatile currents as in the fashion world.

Nevertheless, we believe that French graphic design will continue to promote its most genuine concepts. Looking at a field of work highly illustrative of the French savoir-faire, many luxury brands have recently put the spotlight on French artists, by combining their characterful artistic expressions with these firms' history and expertise. For example, Hermès and Louis Vuitton have respectively collaborated with French illustrator Ugo Gattoni and art director Yorgo Tloupas. Some brands also choose to highlight and re-explore disappearing artisanal techniques, such as ceramics, screen printing and even gilding.

Certainly, graphic design institutions such as M/M Paris, Frédéric Teschner Studio and Helmo, among many others, have contributed a great deal to the 'French attitude' as what the world perceives in French graphics today. Designers and design lovers, and the French in particular, can rely on them, as well as the emerging designers, as a beacon of French creative approach. With the defining features and the historical wealth French graphics contain, we can keep on anticipating how the 'French attitude' would evolve through time.

CONTENTS

42
Creative talents from France

Over the pages, you will get to know both established and emerging creatives who have been actively shaping visual culture in the domains of music, fashion, food, luxury goods and publishing from France. Their diverse body of work covers typography, digital art, illustration, graphics, photography and set design that celebrate their identity, heritage and global culture at once.

Adrienne
Bornstein

Graphics
Paris

Fascinated by typography, design and crafts, Adrienne Bornstein is ceaselessly in search of new expressions and new techniques to produce modern expressions. After nine years of collaboration as an associate at agency Bornstein & Sponchiado, Bornstein decided to go on her own as an independent graphic designer in 2014. Over the years, her projects have touched on visual identity, signage designs, event marketing and publishing projects created for cultural and institutional clients from both public and private sectors.

01 / 4BI & Associés Visual Identity,
2015. Metallic monogram and the
colour red highlight the interior
design agency's practice and close
link with China in recent years.

Can you tell us something about your creations?

I try to have a sensitive approach to my work. Despite the constraints given from the project brief, I want my work to be relevant and punchy, with an artistic and poetic edge.

How would you identify your artistic style with French culture?

I feel like I belong to the young European generation of graphic designers who all share similar knowledge, professional backgrounds and are only differentiated in terms of cultural references. French may be more 'literary' in typography by playing more with line breaks and vintage typefaces.

How do you usually get yourself ready to create?

I always start from the end. By listening to my clients' instructions, I immediately plunge into a certain mood and imagine how the final object or the image is going to look like physically. What kind of emotions does it convey? Does it fit my client's expectation? Then I project myself into a chromatic and typographic universe that heads towards something colourful and contrasting, or lighter and sweeter.

What makes you stay in France?

Over a year ago, I've decided to take full advantage of my life in Paris and create my own design studio here. Clients become my friends. It's easier to develop a close relationship when we share the same cultural codes and sense of humour. Plus I'm unfortunately not adventurous, and don't know if I would feel fine being away from France and Paris.

Where can you find inspiring influences in France?

I'm greatly influenced by objects and images that surround me, from childhood memories to recent finds. I often include in my composition the vintage objects that I've bought in French flea markets.

How would you define French creativity?

France has always been very respectful for its patrimony in all fields. That's why we're still influenced by the likes of Savignac, Bernard Villemot and Cassandre, and appealed by the 'handmade' nature of Michel Bouvet, Philippe Apeloig and Michal Batory's work. However, communications related to mass culture here is still visual-led without much marketing strategies as they are in the States. It's still difficult to differentiate advertising for cultural, car and luxury goods.

What kind of creative practice would you consider unorthodox in the country?

Computerised creations. I was a jury member for schools and have seen young students producing sensitive, high quality graphic design while perfectly mastering the graphic innovations that come out of the coding they created.

What do you plan to do next?

I'm currently working with a product designer. It allows me to discover innovative supports and materials that could lead to the design of 3D graphic objects. I'd also like to work with contemporary artists, using images more than typography to illustrate their reflections and their emotions. It's a field where designers can have more freedom.

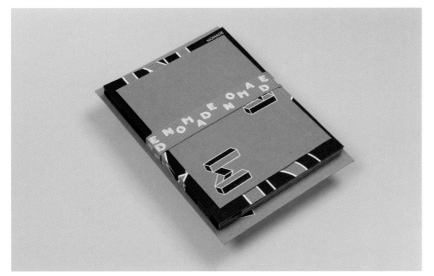

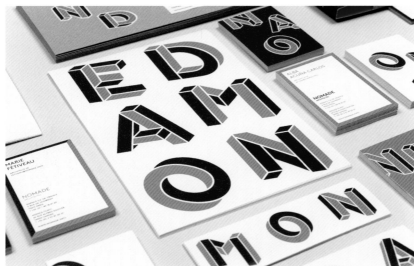

02 / Nomade Architects
Visual Identity, 2014. Adaptable
typography-based identity suite
rendered in Nomade's corporate
colours. Created in hands with
Pierre Sponchiado (p.190) under
Bornstein & Sponchiado.

03 / Front de mode Visual Identity, 2015. Design compares the concept store's eco pursuit with May 1968 events. Blue hints at its founder and owner of fashion brand, Sakina M'Sa.

04 / Studio 02 Architectes Visual identity, 2014. Scalable monograms
and bespoke typeface project SO2's unique character onto its communications. Created in hands with Pierre Sponchiado (p.190) under
Bornstein & Sponchiado.

Akatre

Art direction, typography, installation
Paris

Founded by Valentin Abad, Julien Dhivert and Sébastien Riveron in 2007, Akatre works across the disciplines of graphic design, photography, typography, video and artistic installations that acknowledge and re-explore traditional crafts in contemporary ways. Their portfolio is recently complete with music productions, which they compose and perform in-house to complement their video clips. Regular clients include cultural institutions, luxury brands, fashion and magazines.

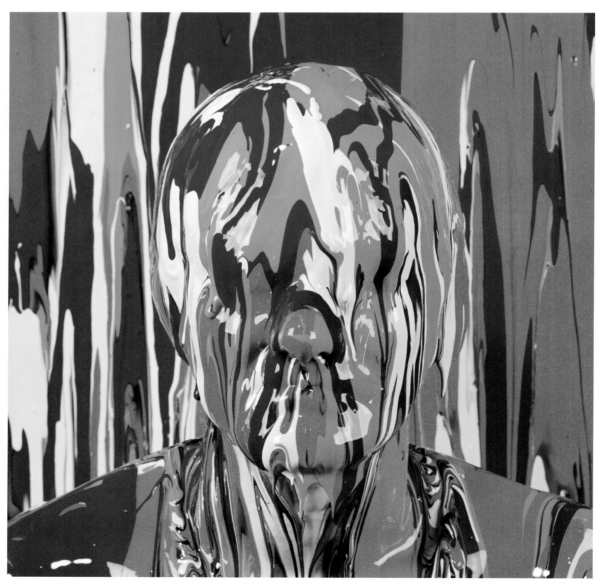

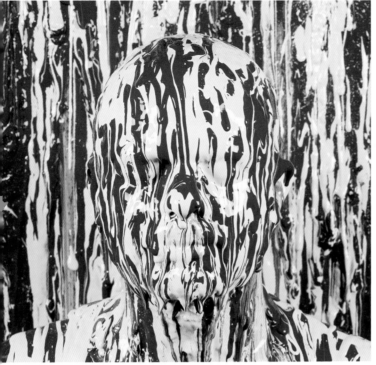

01 / T O G O B A N, 2014. Cover
art for QDRPD's album, T O G
O B A N.

Can you tell us something about your creations?

We create complete universes with no lack of humour or malice, and by transforming everyday objects, we take away their set function to exploit their visual qualities.

How would you identify your artistic style with French culture?

We don't specifically feel French when we produce a design. We think that we have to create something the way we want it to be, and not align ourselves with a specific style or our culture.

How do you usually get yourself ready to create?

Coffee, tea and good food is our only one routine. Our desks are always full of paper and our bottles of water.

What makes you stay in France?

We work in France because we haven't had the opportunity to work abroad yet. We would love to work in other countries, to meet people and discover other cultures.

How would you define French creativity?

We think that French creativity stands out in cinema, animated films, gastronomy and music. We are fortunate to have a magnificent and diverse theatre, both in its production and distribution. We have the world of cinema that comes to us and is looking at us. It's an incredible opportunity that is often overlooked. We are excited about this luck. Art direction in French animated films is popular and inspires the world. It's true in video games too. French gastronomy is a pride that inspires us, just like contemporary and classical dance, for its rigorous nature and creativity. Music is essential for us, because we work all day in music. To us, independent music bands are more creative and interesting than that we can hear everywhere.

What kind of creative practice would you consider unorthodox in the country?

Perhaps graphic design, because this professional practice is still not receiving enough respect in France. Graphic designers aren't considered a "proper profession" like [fashion/product] designers and artists.

What do you plan to do next?

We want to do a lot of things, like magazines, films, music, more exhibitions, product design, or music performances. Now we are working on a personal and experimental publishing project we hold dear and we would like to collaborate with an editor on it. The soundtrack of our Museum of Decorative Arts exhibition "Recto Verso: 8 pièces graphiques" is also in progress alongside some other very different tracks. Other than that, video making is a field that we wish to invest as much effort into as we did for our photographic projects.

02

03

04

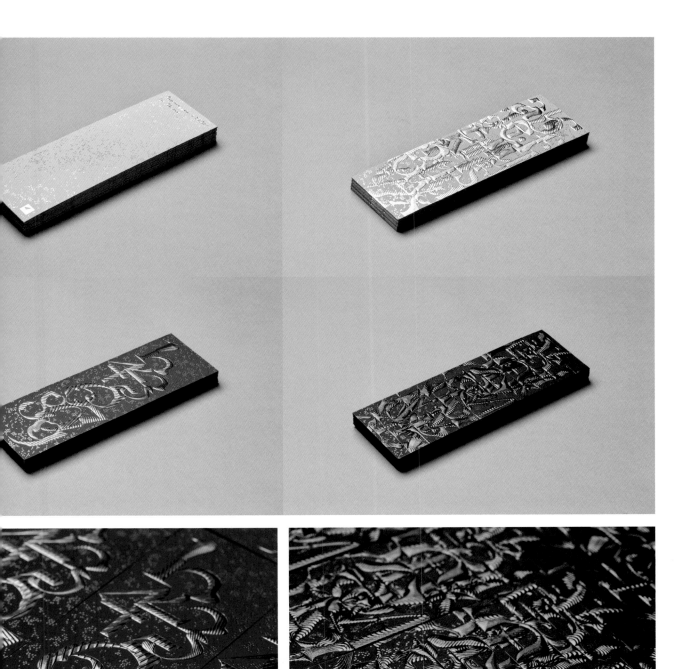

05

02-04 / Album cover art &
typography. In numerical order:
Aaron - We cut the night (2015),
Øliver - Fortune cookies (2015),
Benjamin Clementine - At Least
for Now (2015).

05 / Arjowiggins x Fiac by
Akatre, 2015. Bookmarks for
the Fiac catalogue made with
Arjowiggins papers.

06

07

08

09

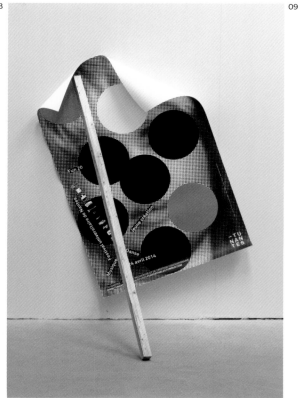

06 / EKLEROSHOCK, 2015. Visual for Ekleroshock Label night at
Nuba, Paris.

07-08 / TU Nantes visuals, 2014-
15. Ice Cream kicks off season
15/16. TU Nantes 2014 marked
the beginning of season 14/15.

09 / Fun 20, 2014. Poster design
for a TU Nantes event.

10 / STUDIO 13/16, 2015. Visual
celebrates studio 13/16's 5th
anniversary.

Alexia Roux

Graphics
Montpellier

Born in Béziers and currently based in Montpellier, Alexia Roux has been in the graphic design industry since 2009 and is very attached to the relations between graphic objects and space. A graduate of the Lycée des Arènes in Toulouse, Roux has developed a special sensitivity to materials and graphic-spatial arrangements that essentially shapes her approach to visual identity projects and print designs. Her other skills lie in art direction and web design.

Can you tell us something about your creations?

I am very attached to layout design in the editorial sense. My graphic design training has increased my sensitivity to the materiality of printed objects — how they're connected with their functions, the occasion which they function and their relation to the object itself. The choice of materials essentially informs my concepts in every aspect.

How would you identify your artistic style with French culture?

I really don't have an objective view on my work. I just make things the way I feel about it.

How do you usually get yourself ready to create?

I always draft repeatedly on paper before really starting to work. It's nothing conventional, not in a copybook or on white clear paper, but my agenda or a price tag. I love to start without pressure. I don't draw well but ideas come to me when I draw or write, especially for logo designs and identities. After that I build on my drafts on the computer. Often I start to work once I receive the first enquiry.

What makes you stay in France?

I love the freedom my south-of-France lifestyle gives me and having my family not far away from me makes me feel great and creative. We live in a small city but I appreciate that I can just take my car and go to the beach in 30 minutes, go to the mountains or see my parents. I can visit Marseille and Toulouse in two hours for a change of culture. My south-of-France lifestyle is a mix between the Mediterranean and old country way of life. That being said, I would still like to travel more for new discoveries and broaden my vision.

Where can you find inspiring influences in France?

I can especially find inspirations at home, or at my family's home. When I am back to my basics I have just one thing to think — to make what I want.

How would you define French creativity?

For me, "le style a la française" can be defined as "elegant".

What do you plan to do next?

I want to work with more places and spaces, especially with French chefs and their restaurants. Even if I don't cook I love food and restaurants. It's a pleasure to work with creative French chefs like Pierre Augé (my local hero, after my dad and grandpa). Taking pictures and creating for someone who have their own artistic universe is really interesting.

01 / *HÉMISPHÈRE brand identity,*
2015. Horizontal line cuts the
name in half to indicate the two
Montpellier stores that stock
women's and men's gear.

02 / *MANIFEST brand identity,*
2015. Business card's recycled
cardboard reflects the industrial
aesthetics that characterise the
lifestyle store's interior space.

03 / *Le Quotidien des Tranchees,*
2015. A project on smell as a sign
of invasion in war zones. Smell
exudes as ink being soaked up
blotting paper.

04 / *INCENDIE, 2015. Book*
design with burnt marks to raise
awareness of Cassis forest fires
in 2010.

03

Antoine+ Manuel

Graphics, scenography
Paris

Antoine+Manuel is Antoine Audiau (b. Paris) and Manuel Warosz (b. Clermont-Ferrand). Since 1993, the duo has made a name for themselves by occupying the industry's foreground, which lead to collaborations and long-standing relationships with the broad creative industries, including prestigious dance companies in and outside France. Brands like Cartier, Yves Saint Laurent, Uniqlo, Nike and Christian Lacroix have shown approval of their work. Audiau and Warosz become members of the Alliance Graphique Internationale in 2012. Portrait by Valérie Le Guern (Atelier de Sèvres).

02

03

01 / Uzès danse, 2015. Poster for the dance festival on its 20th anniversary.

02 / Une saison danse, 2012. Poster for the dance season programme at CNDC, Angers.

03 / Schools is cools!, 2011. Poster for a schools dance festival at CNDC, Angers.

Can you tell us something about your creations?

We like to work on new and challenging projects where our creativity could be experimented with maximum freedom. Experimenting new approaches with different materials and techniques is part of our creative process, like having new rules to play a game. It could be a manual process like painting or a digital one such as moving images. Most of the time our projects are set in 3D. As a duo we of course have our own favourite tools and softwares, Manuel is more into vector and Antoine more pixel.

How would you identify your artistic style with French culture?

We don't see the difference of design between different cultures, but like cuisine it's a balance between chosen ingredients which at the end should be pleasurably eaten.

How do you usually get yourself ready to create?

We usually start by drawing before we computerised it to enhance or transform it. We call it a 'digital DIY approach'. But we also listen to music and cook in the studio every day.

What makes you stay in France?

After school we started working in Paris and decided to start a studio. It was easy to stay here as we love our city, and maybe we're too lazy to move elsewhere.

Where can you find inspiring influences in France?

Everywhere from art exhibitions to disco, from food market to books…

How would you define French creativity?

Courageous and inventive.

What kind of creative practice would you consider unorthodox in the country?

Fashion, art, design and performing arts. Everywhere where creativity is free and strong.

What do you plan to do next?

Each new project is always very exciting. We recently started exploring video projection installation and we want to continue with this on a greater scale. Our latest project is the visual identity for Villa Noailles in Hyères, a place where fashion, photography and design are the keywords.

04 / *Abonnez-vous!, 2013. Poster for the season programme at La Comédie de Clermont-Ferrand National Theater.*

05 / *Abonnez-vous!, 2014. Brochure cover and poster for the season programme at La Comédie de Clermont-Ferrand National Theater.*

04

05

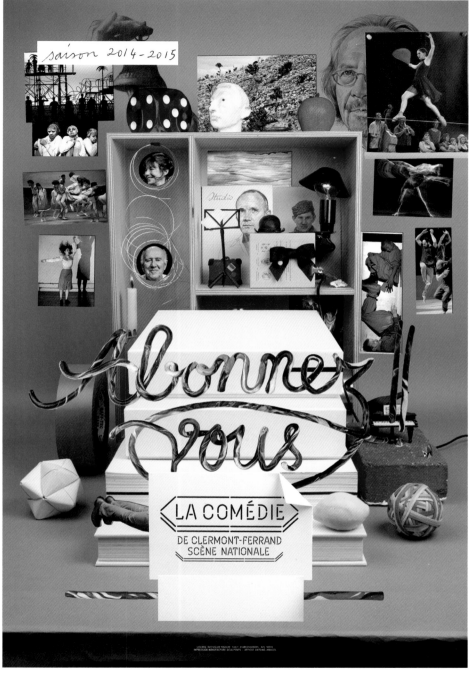

06 / Cartieroscope (Café Society), 2013. A 135-metre-wide 24-minute animated projection for the Salon d'Honneur of the Grand Palais at exhibition "Cartier, le style et l'histoire".

07 / Capsula, 2014. Wooden cabin installation doubles as a projection room built for exhibition "Les Fils du Calvaire" at the Chapelle des Calvairiennes Art Center, Mayenne.

08 / Schools 3, 2013. Poster for a schools dance festival at CNDC, Angers.

09 / Abonnez-vous!, 2015. Poster for the season programme at La Comédie de Clermont-Ferrand National Theater.

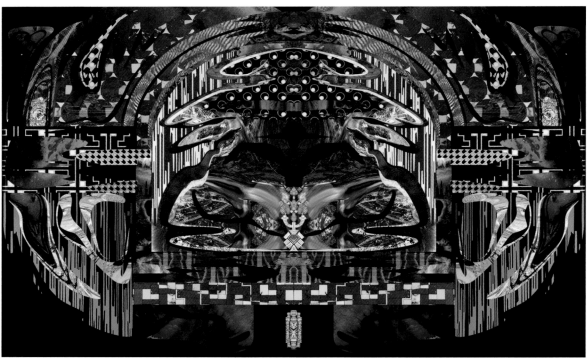

06

07

08

09

Artworklove

Art direction, graphics
Paris

Founded in 2009, Artworklove approaches design as artistic experimentation with emphasis on concept execution, finish and a balance between functions and forms. The studio's specialities lie in art directions, visual branding and print design. Cultural institutions and high-end brands such as Barbican Art Gallery, Chloé Parfums and Champagne Krug had approached AWL for exhibition identities, product launch campaigns, packaging and promotional communication designs.

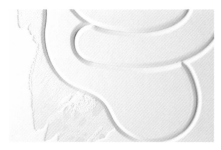

Can you tell us something about your creations?

We like to create unexpected, intriguing and timeless designs. Each of our project tends to create emotional and poetic connections and often has a playful dimension to it. We don't follow trends. We avoid pastiche and push the boundaries every time to produce designs that are truly technically innovative, especially in print.

How would you identify your artistic style with French culture?

We don't have a definite style. There is no formula to what we do and there is no repetition. We constantly move forward and go for the best solution for each commission as we explore our own creative power and estimate the public's emotional connection with our work. At the same time, we make sure the solution is adequate for the brief.

How do you usually get yourself ready to create?

I always begin with cleaning up my desk before taking out a new blank sheet or notebook. I love to sketch out my ideas and jot down the impulsive ones that first come to mind. The most interesting part is when the blurred edges take shape and become concrete ideas.

What makes you stay in France?

The life I lead here and the connections I've made over the years make me very attached to the place. I feel I've struck the perfect work-life balance here. Paris is also an incredibly dynamic and cultural city.

Where can you find inspiring influences in France?

Chaumont and Offprint to name two independent festivals for graphic design, photography and book publishing.

How would you define French creativity?

It is free and less impaired by commercialism than in other countries. The peculiarity probably allows it to be more expressive and have a unique style that is very French in a way.

What kind of creative practice would you consider unorthodox in the country?

In fact I don't think there is any art practice I would consider unorthodox today! The word 'unorthodox' is quite strong. However we do have a few French people and studios in mind that we love and are proud of. Many of them create interesting and inspiring projects, like Arnold Goron, Atelier Tout va bien, Fanette Mellier, Leslie David, Violaine & Jérémy, My name is, gr20paris, The Shelf Journal, Holiday magazine by Atelier Franck Durand, Back Cover, Charlotte Cheetham, Atelier Müesli, CLEOBURO and many others.

What do you plan to do next?

We're experimenting embroidered graphics on paper, working on a museum website for a Parisian haute couture brand and an identity for a palace in south of France, to name a few.

— *Marion Laurens, Art director of Artworklove*

01 / Imprimerie du Marais Invitation, 2015. Invitations
and souvenir items for Imprimerie's Pack & Gift Fair
showcase the printer's specialised ateliers, printing
techniques and tools.

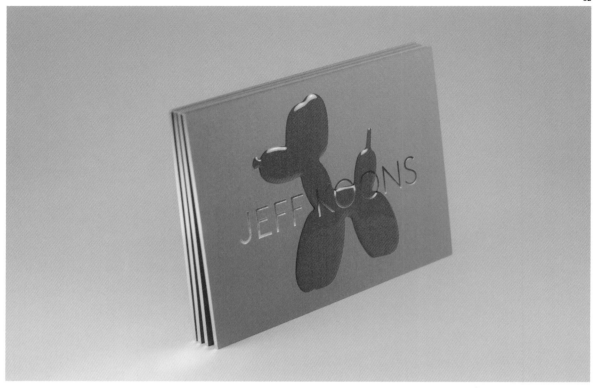

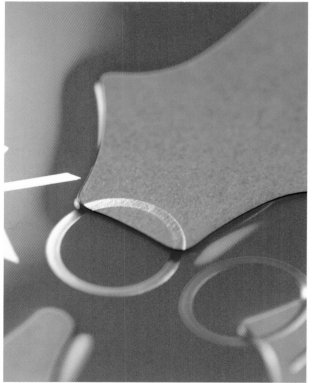

02 / Jeff Koons, 2015. Invitation for a private dinner and visit to Jeff Koons's exhibition at the Centre Pompidou. Commissioned by Bouygues Bouygues Bâtiment Ile-de-France.

03 / Picasso.Mania, 2015. Invitation for a private dinner and exhibition visit, suggestive of Pablo Picasso's great stylistic phases and iconic works. Commissioned by Bouygues Bouygues Bâtiment Ile-de-France.

03

atelier bingo.

Illustration
Saint-Laurent-sur-Sèvre

Comprised of illustrators Adèle Favreau from Cholet and Maxime Prou from Nantes, atelier bingo. shares a consuming passion for patterns, colours and screenprints. Forsaking city life after two years of working in Paris upon their graduation in Nante, the duo decided to opt for a rural life and create wonderful abstract collage art in the Vendée countryside in an old factory building. Today, the duo's portfolio is a delightful blend of client work and personal projects, ranging from art zines, illustrations and prints.

01 / *Pink-Blue-Green Floral*
Abstract, 2014. Greetings Cards
for Wrap Magazine.

Can you tell us something about your creations?

We are two illustrator/graphic designer who love to experiment with paper-cutting and screenprinting to create colourful and abstract works. We like to collaborate with clients and find a way to translate the "bingo. Style" upon their requests! Our clients include Vogue, Sosh, Pull & Bear, Wanderlust, CALEPINO, Wrap Magazine, Farfetch, FEATHR, ILADO, GUR, The Plant, The Loop, Aelfie and more.

How would you identify your artistic style with French culture?

The children of Henri Matisse.

How do you usually get yourself ready to create?

We always start the day with coffee, cutting paper together and looking for shapes and colours afterwards with laughter! We're always waiting for the bingo moment while creating the composition. We do a lot of screenprintng as well because the act of creation helps us think and move further rather than just sitting on our desk for work.

What makes you stay in France?

Maxime speaks only French, so maybe for that. And maybe for the food too.

Where can you find inspiring influences in France?

In the countryside, you are quite influenced by the colours of the seasons. Apart from that, we really like to visit the Emmaus store next to our house. It's full of vintage stuff with crazy graphic design.

How would you define French creativity?

A lot of know-how and knowledge have been gathered in creative fields through time. We just hope that they won't disappear in the years to come.

What kind of creative practice would you consider unorthodox in the country?

We really love the work of Calepino. They create amazing and beautiful notebooks in Nantes, and print some of them in letterpress. On the contrary, we dislike cliché designs with the Eiffel tower or an image of a French guy with a baguette under his arm.

What do you plan to do next?

We really want to try ceramics and painting! But we will give it time, we are young.

02 / Vegetal Party, 2014. Illustrations depict a jungle of plants to company an interview for Wrap Magazine #10, themed "Into the Wild".

03 / The Patriotic Sunday, 2015. Cover art made from collages, illustration and graphic design for folk pop group's album "All I Can't Forget", released by Murailles Music.

04 / Wogoo Zoogi, 2014. Visual-isation of an abstract discussion between two aliens for a 16-page book riso-printed by Tan & Loose Press. Done in collaboration with Tan & Loose Press.

02

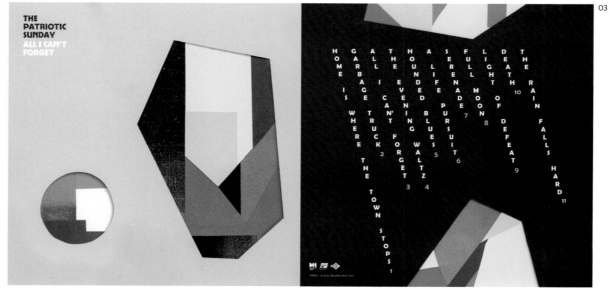

03

THE
PATRIOTIC
SUNDAY
ALL I CAN'T
FORGET

04

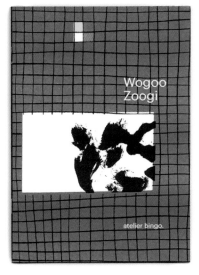

Wogoo
Zoogi

atelier bingo.

Atelier
Tout va bien

Graphics
Dijon

Anna Chevance (b. Dijon) and Mathias Reynoird (b. Angers) know right away that graphic design is where their hearts belong after their diploma study at the École Européenne Supérieure d'Art de Bretagne (ÉESAB) in Rennes. Since founding Atelier Tout va bien in 2011, the French duo has been transferring their love of forms, lines and colours into meaningful messages for cultural and corporate clients. Whether it's poster design or book design, Tout va bien's graphic sensibility stands out in spatial arrangements, lettering and colour choices.

01

Can you tell us something about your creations?

We apply a three-level acknowledgement system to both our commissioned and personal print-based projects: Perception, Readability and Reflection. 'Perception' appeals to viewers' senses such as sight and touch, as well as their consequent feelings. 'Readability' means the result has to be crystal clear for viewers to understand, receive information and remember. Lastly, we try to let viewers take a stand and to be critical on a subject. We call this concept 'Reflection' which often articulates everything together and make our work much more interesting.

How would you identify your artistic style with French culture?

We hope to creative with no specific style, whether or not it's connected with French culture. Our goal is to adapt our design to the specificity of each new demand.

How do you usually get yourself ready to create?

A good freshly brewed coffee and a croissant!

What makes you stay in France?

We like the fact that everyday is a challenge in France. We were both quite impressed to discover that our profession receives more respect in Germany and the Netherlands during our internship. We would love to see that happen in France. Somehow we try to educate our clients about the possibilities of graphic design brick by brick. We choose to

settle in Burgundy as culture is still a less coveted domain here. Other reasons include its wine, cheese and of course the great atmosphere!

Where can you find inspiring influences in France?

It is important for us to find inspiration and balance from everything around us outside of the atelier, whether it's the colour of the beautiful nature, the cover of a dusty LP at the flea market, a detail crafted in a sculpture or the red wine we have ever tasted. We believe that finding this balance is extremely important.

How would you define French creativity?

There's no such thing as French creativity. There are simply lots of good designers. You cannot put all eggs in one basket, especially when the internet continues to expand the borders of design.

What kind of creative practice would you consider unorthodox in the country?

Despite our preference for print, web development and design are the ones you should always keep an eye on, mainly because of the technological frenzy we are going through. In fact, all creative practices are constantly changing and evolving, and we hope to keep getting surprised!

What do you plan to do next?

Besides helping people with interesting projects, we need to find the time to design a new website and make major updates regarding our projects. Designing more books is also a goal for the next few years.

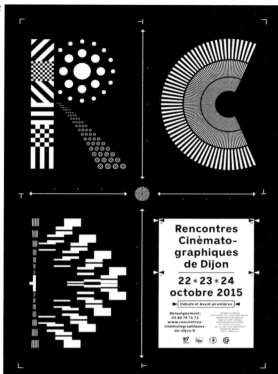

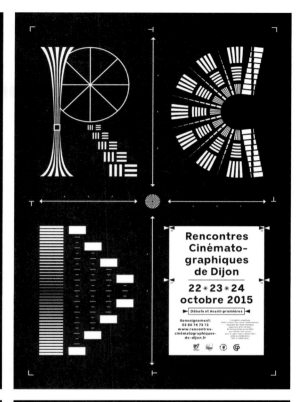

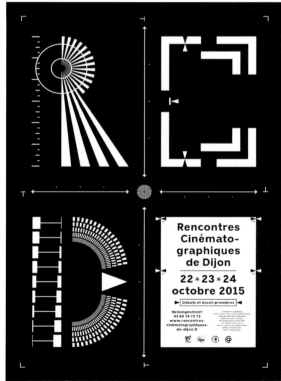

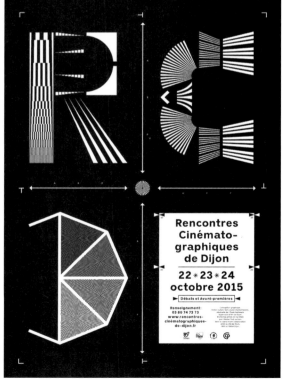

01-02 / Les Rencontres Cinématographiques de Dijon, 2015.
Visual identity and posters draw on the graphic vocabulary
of NBS test chart (mire de Foucault) to reflect on French
movie productions through letters "R", "C", "D".

03

*03 / L'Orange mécanique, 2015.
Duotone silkscreen poster uses
"type as stripes" as the graphic
base to illustrate the key scenes
of the novel Clockwork Orange
for Compagnie Esquimots.*

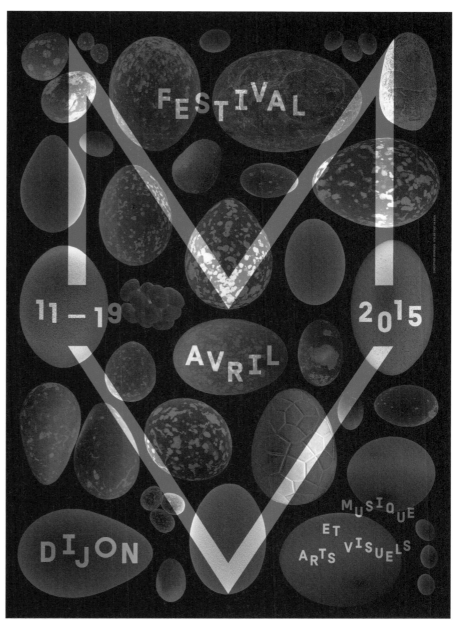

04

05

04 / Open doors isdaT, 2015. Duotone silkscreen poster highlights the five different courses offered by L'institut supérieur des arts de Toulouse (isdaT).

05 / Festival MV, 2015. Duotone silkscreen poster for the second Festival MV responds to the visuals of the first festival. The eggs are what remain after the birds left last time's event.

06 / Une promenade, 2013. Photography book de-
fies the form of books and invites readers to explore
the photographic inserts for artist Harald Fernagu.
Photo: Daniele Mendini for Fedrigoni

07 / Les bœufs Vaporetto, 2014·15. Duotone riso
print invitations present the monthly music adven-
tures at venue Vaporetto in forms of vibrations,
balances and rhythms.

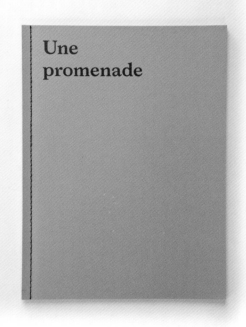

BŒUFS

JEUDI 30 OCT. 2014

LA VAPEUR

BŒUFS

JEUDI 04 DÉC. 2014

LA VAPEUR

BŒUFS

JEUDI 12 MARS 2015

LA VAPEUR

BŒUFS

JEUDI 7 MAI 2015

LA VAPEUR

BŒUFS

JEUDI 21 MAI 2015

LA PÉNICHE CANCALE

BŒUFS

JEUDI 18 JUIN 2015

LA VAPEUR

Avant
Post

Art direction, graphics
Paris

Before setting up Avant Post in 2014, Quentin Berthelot, Johan Mossé and Adrien Weibel have already been collaborating under Collectif 5M and freelancing at the same time, from Marseille and Paris, for clients from both public and private domains. Their creative bond has been there since the three studied at École de Communication Visuelle (ECV) in Provence and can be identified by strong concepts, combined with photography and digital art. Particular attention to type arrangements adds to the studio's creative approach.

01

Can you tell us something about your creations?

Our goal is to develop strong creative concepts and translate them into minimalist designs. We give particular attention to typography, creating specific typefaces that fit the project. We also develop photographic concepts. The combination of these two elements often enhances the concept while keeping the outcome visually clean.

How would you identify your artistic style with French culture?

We do not entirely identify ourselves with French culture. To us, French graphic design style is more about creating strong images, whereas we work towards being 'information architects' who develop concepts through organising elements within a graphic system that we design. This is why French designers influence us as much as Dutch or Swiss studios do.

What makes you stay in France?

We grew up in the French Riviera, but decided to launch our studio in Paris. Our best creative opportunities often come from the fashion industry and cultural institutions, and Paris is a cultural hub where we can develop such collaborations as well as a variety of other projects.

Where can you find inspiring influences in France?

Both in the works of great designers and the amateur creations that we stumble upon in the streets, such as the handpainted typefaces of Paris' classic storefronts. We try to spot little details that we could use in a smart way when they fit the creative concept.

How would you define French creativity?

This is a really tricky question. We can define our own creativity process, but it would be unrealistic to pretend that we understand what French creativity is. Does such a thing exist? On our level, we consider ourselves part artists part craftsmen who try to keep a good balance between our will to create and the need to deliver efficient designs.

What kind of creative practice would you consider unorthodox in the country?

French fashion brand Andrea Crews' interesting use of typography and patterns by great graphic designers in the recent collection exercises impressive visual creativity. Also, packaging of supermarket Monoprix, designed exclusively with typefaces, clever use of colour and humorous jokes, has put the potential of typography into full use. The link between words and typography is a powerful tool that is still rarely used in France, where people seem to be more attached to images.

What do you plan to do next?

When we graduated, we were all about print design. We still love print, but we also developed digital projects and photography direction. We would like to continue that way, extending the fields of application of our creativity to for example motion design, movies direction and so on. We think it's the best way to never get into a routine.

01 / Stop départ, 2014. Photographic series and postcard design depicts motifs of the start of an athletic race to hint the studio's ambition of gunning for gold. Photo by Samuel Guigues.

02 / Tchikebe, 2012. Logo, visual identity and custom typeface for Tchikebe, a screenprinting workshop in Marseille. Co-created with Anaïs Bourdet.

03-04 / Phonopaca, 2014-15. Album cover art for two annual compilations of the Federation of Independent Record Labels, PACA region.

02

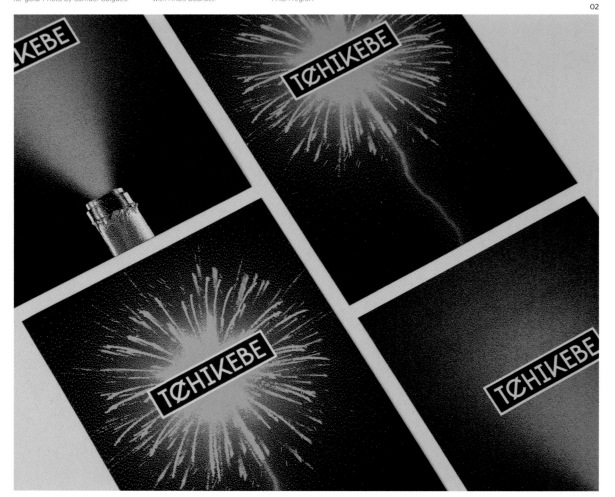

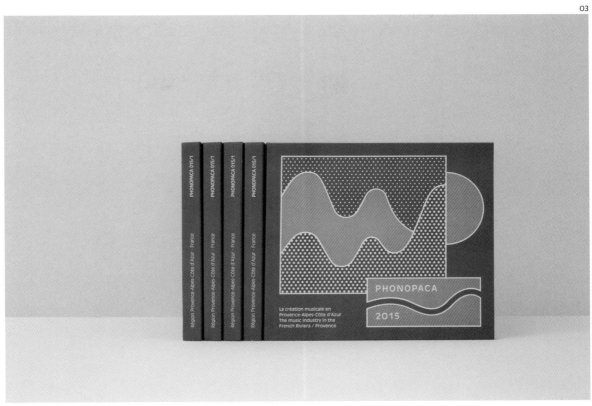

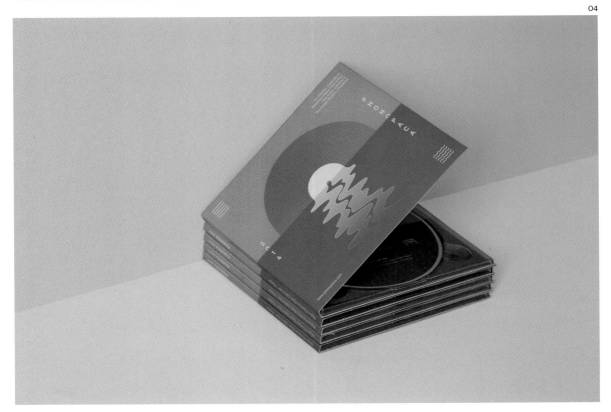

05 / Les Salins, 2014. Visual identity, printed programme and poster design for the theatre season. Co-created with Anaïs Bourdet.

06 / Les Salins, 2015. Annual and quarterly poster design for the theatre based the "four seasons" theme. Photo by Samuel Guigues.

05

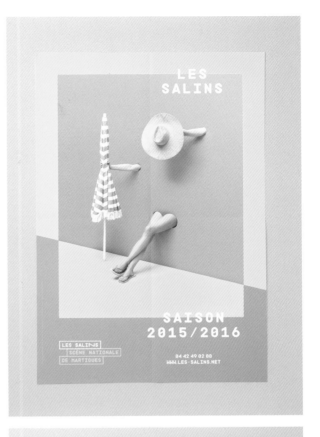

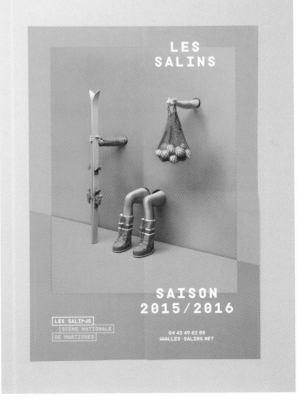

Benoit Challand

Digital art
Lyon

Born in Marseille, bred in Provence and schooled in Lyon, Benoit Challand started out as a digital art director in 2009. Specialising in 3D rendering, CGI design and digital art, Challand has worked at agencies like Publicis, Anonymous (Paris) and Serialcut (Madrid) before going on his own. Where Challand's early career was mostly about web and animation design, he's recently on creating 3D still visuals marked by remarkable details and compositions. Portrait by Jean-Baptiste Sinniger.

Can you tell us something about your creations?

I focus on 3D illustration, design and art direction, which encompass diverse creative disciplines like set design, animation, digital art and more. I like to put myself in creative and dynamic environments where ideas have no limits. I find inspiration in everything that surrounds me such as art, graphic and industrial design, architecture, photography, new technologies, etc.

How would you identify your artistic style with French culture?

I guess my work can be defined as 3D art. I'm from a little town in the south of France. I grew up with engravers, cabinetmakers, blacksmiths and carvers where techniques, tools and experience give birth to a creation. My creative background was built by the likes of Le Corbusier and Victor Vasarely. I came to 3D art because beyond an obvious form of expression like graphics, I can create more extravagant shapes.

How do you usually get yourself ready to create?

I need a lot of music so I'll start by setting up a good playlist and wear my headphones to be 100% focused on my work. I do look for inspiration from books and magazines but most of the time I search the internet.

What makes you stay in France?

France is a really good place in Europe as it sticks to six other countries. It's an open gate to top notch creative cities like London, Barcelona and Berlin. I worked one year in Madrid and used to move around for inspirations.

Where can you find inspiring influences in France?

French has a diverse legacy as well as contemporary art. You can find a six-metre high street art painted alongside cathedrals, or a massive egg-shaped rock of Andy Goldsworthy in the middle of a village in southern France. You can find inspiration in architecture, design, fashion, street art, food, shop and so on.

How would you define French creativity?

I can't define French creativity in one word. I prefer to say that lots of French artists inspire me and I consider some of them genius: Möbius, Victor Vasarely (not French-born but he lived in France all his life), Roger Tallon, Georges Rousse, the DMV crew to name a few.

What do you plan to do next?

I would love to experiment with 3D real-time and virtual reality experiences.

01 / Pen Orchestra, 2014. A personal project that plays around with pens.

02 / Furniture, 2014. A personal project on "fun constructivism".

03 / Vinopole, 2014. A set of illustrations created as posters for the Vinochromie exhibition in Paris.

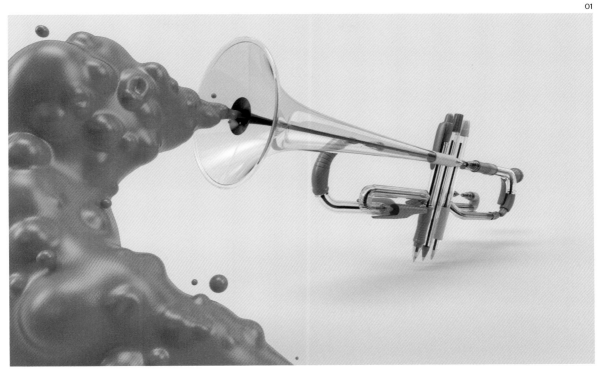

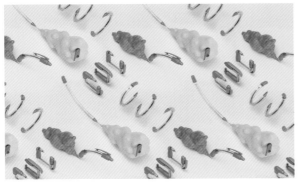

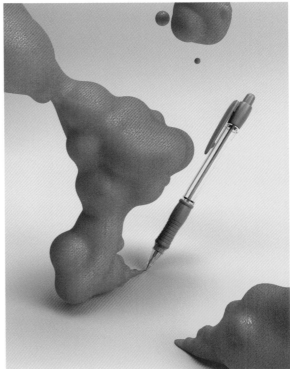

BONSOIR PARIS

Art direction, scenography
Paris

Born out of a love for breaking limits, BONSOIR PARIS promotes new perspectives through restless experimentation and innovative techniques. Founded and led by creative directors Rémy Clémente and Morgan Maccari, the creative studio boggles minds with an all-media approach where graphics, sculpture, scenography and digital experiences blur the lines between commerce, art and science. Their daring play of strange materials match logic to absurdity across fashion editorials, retail spaces and brand campaigns.

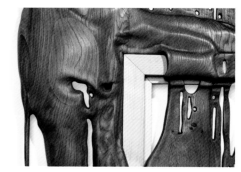

Can you tell us something about your creations?

We are a creative studio that works in the domains of artistic direction, spatial and object design, experiential installations, photography and filmmaking. This scope is brought together through a focus on experimentation and innovative techniques, explored in the intersection of art, design and technology.

How would you identify your artistic style with French culture?

While we are well rooted in our namesake city, we do not particularly identify our artistic style with French culture, but rather a broad set of inspiration from around the world — be it the architectural poetry of Tadao Ando from Japan, or the experiential installations of Icelandic-Danish artist Olafur Eliasson. That being said, French and European savoir-faire is core to our studio, as we work with a local network of skilled artisans, engineers and fabricators to produce our designs.

What makes you stay in France?

Our foundation and roots are based in this country, as both our founders are French and have lived in Paris for over two decades. Our third partner, Ben, came to this country for its artistic prowess and cultural influence, deciding to stay close to the pulse of city's creative centres in design, fashion and advertising.

Where can you find inspiring influences in France?

France is historically (and not incorrectly) seen as a patrimony replete with institutions of art, fashion and design, so there are many opportunities to find influence here. Beyond simply living in the centre of quotidian influence, we find interacting, collaborating with our creative cohorts in this city (and abroad) keep us inspired, keen to experiment and exchange with the talented network of creatives around us.

How would you define French creativity?

The wealth of French creativity is rooted in the country's principles of social collaboration and mutual understanding, as well as the multitude of international influencers arriving at Paris, constituted by designers, artists, musicians and creative entrepreneurs.

What kind of creative practice would you consider unorthodox in the country?

Cross media collaboration made possible by the democratisation of technology is perhaps the most innovative creative practice — mixing methods in innovative ways, like mathematics, paramedic design and music videos, as well as robotics and set design.

What do you plan to do next?

Our studio will focus on the creation of new technologies and tools that computation and robotics give us. We'll also keep on exploring boundaries between image making and design applications. We'll devote more time to collaborations with both designers and image makers to share our vision on both creation paths.

01 / Duramen, 2011. A handmade wooden sculpture series. Deformed frames represent the wish to break away from the conventional ways of exhibiting. Photo by Davina Muller.

01

03 / Frame, 2015. Photographic
series and cover image for
Frame magazine #105.

03

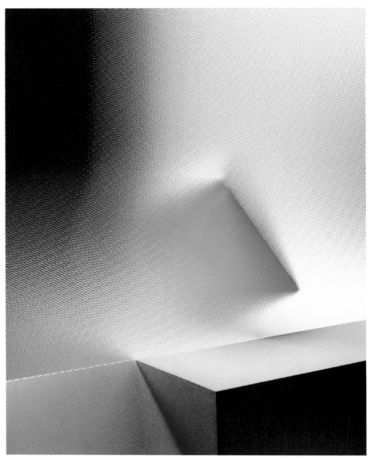

04 / *Bright Young Things, 2013. Window installation and pop-up concept store for Selfridges London's annual "Bright Young Things" initiative. Photo by Andrew Meredith.*

04

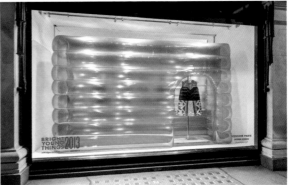

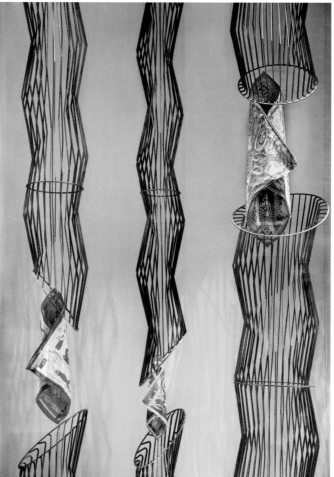

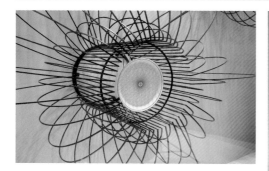

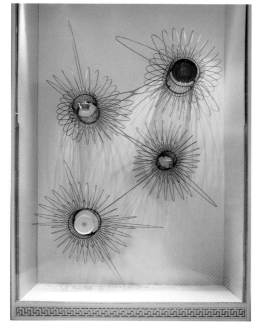

BONSOIR PARIS

街の愛こんばんは愛の街

& BEN SANDLER PRESENT

#1

画像

ここに

あそ

YANN BOUSSSAND LARCHER メイクアップアーティスト メイクアップアーティスト メイクアップアーティスト

モデル JANE ヘアスタイリスト @ FORD CHIAO CHENET TALENT

KEVIN ROSA アシスタント

BONSOIR PARIS アートディレクション

JEAN-PAUL PAULA スタイリスト BEN SANDLER フォトグラファー

A FASHION STORY FOR METAL MAGAZINE
メタル誌のファッションストーリー

ジャ JAPAN ハン

インターネット上の専用

05 / Hermès Dubai, 2015. Window installation themed "Flaneur Forever" for Hermès Dubai flagship store.

06 / Metal, 2014. Photography and set design for the artist interview series of Daily Metal, Metal magazine's digital platform.

Bureau Kayser

Art direction, graphics
Paris

Established and headed by art director and graphic designer Laure-anne Kayser, Bureau Kayser approaches editorial projects and visual identities with a sharp eye for lettering and image compositions. Their signature style draws upon a sense of reflection, often made possible by collaborating with photographers, and contributes an aura of peace with a contemporary appeal. Kayer's works are driven by an interest in typographic research and experimentation, frequently applied in the communications within the arts and cultural realm.

01 / *All I Ever Wanted*, 2015. Book design for photographer Hester Scheurwater's limited edition photo book, *All I Ever Wanted*. Published by Éditions Bessard.

Can you tell us something about your creations?

I work on print, editorial and interactive designs, identities and branding solutions principally in the fields of art, fashion and culture. I like to create timeless solutions with a strong foundation of reflection and composition. I love experimenting with pictures and textures, destroying or magnifying images. I take time and play with details to propose to my clients the most appropriate solutions.

How would you identify your artistic style with French culture?

I don't feel my work is necessarily linked to the French culture only as I moved and travelled a lot and keep an inquisitive mind. My influences vary. I'm inspired by conceptual art from the 60s, underground culture, Herzog's documentaries, experimental short movies, Ed Ruscha's photographs, the strong and contemporary images of Charlie Engman's blog, pieces of Ettore Sottsass, Le Corbusier architecture, textures in Daisuke Yokota's work, as well as minerals and nature.

How do you usually get yourself ready to create?

First I try to clear my mind entirely. I won't hesitate to walk a lot or do something which has absolutely nothing to do with the project before I begin to create. My office is above a bookstore, so I often take a walk around in the store before I start to work. After that I go up, pick up the tools I need and begin to find ideas with paper, a pen and a coffee.

What makes you stay in France?

I am from Marseille and went to Paris to study at Gobelins Art School. After graduating and gaining experiences in several agencies, I met my 'playmates' and found Bureau Kayser, so I decided to stay in France. It is a rewarding and stimulating country to create in.

Where can you find inspiring influences in France?

The past, for example. These days I am reading *The Form of the Book Book* which contains a text 'Le Corbusier as Book Designer: Semi Modernity à la française' by art historian and critic Catherine de Smet. The piece discusses the French architect's take on editorial production. This kind of analysis can be a real source of inspiration.

How would you define French creativity?

It's difficult to give a definite description. There are as many artists or designers as there are the ways they create in France. Everything is about talent and I think there are a lot of talents in France, of course.

What kind of creative practice would you consider unorthodox in the country?

I love creativity which takes risks or experiments with things. It pushes me to work harder. These types of alternative movements exist in France. I am constantly impressed by the work of other French artists, designers, photographers, architects or musicians. The emergent creations can hold their own and go further.

What do you plan to do next?

We want to further explore photography and art direction.

— *Laure-anne Kayser, Founder of Bureau Kayser*

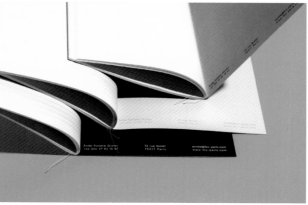

02 / iko x Maud Rémy-Lonvis, 2015. Note-book design for the collaboration between artist agency iko and photographer Maud Rémy-Lonvis.

03 / Cahier OO, 2015. Book
design for photographer Maud
Rémy-Lonvis's limited edition
photo book, Cahier OO.

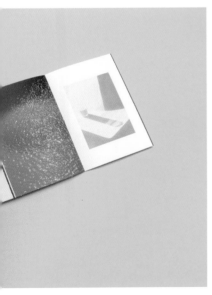

catalogue

Art direction, graphics
Lyon

Graphic designer Gaspard Ollagnon has an agile yet methodical approach to design that lives up to his studio's name, catalogue. From visual identities to editorial layouts and typographic treatments, catalogue answers communication questions with a visual system guided by tested rules that account for the slick and structured results. His father as a dedicated painter, design master Karl Gerstner and Parisian publisher and creative studio deValence have contributed significant influences on Ollagnon's current graphic style.

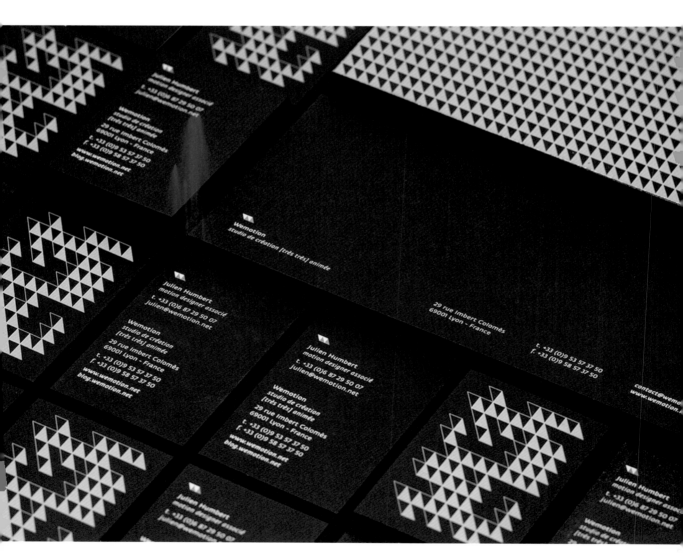

Can you tell us something about your creations?

My work is about addressing communication questions with relevant visual answers — to shape messages. Most of the time I treat my projects, from graphic design, visual identities, scenography to digital projects, as systems. I establish rules that are tested against their efficacy, accuracy and limits. The result of these researches is only one version of a universe of possibilities in respect of established rules. I like to think beyond what has been asked to find their variations. That is how my work makes sense to me and how it allows me to explore new areas in personal projects on the research of rhythm, composition and harmony.

How would you identify your artistic style with French culture?

We now have full access to graphic design and creative productions around the world, so it's hard sometimes to differentiate between what comes from our French identity and what comes from the influences we learn from books and screens.

How do you usually get yourself ready to create?

When it's possible: calm, sleep, space.

What makes you stay in France?

Well, the way of living is nice and French culture is interesting. People also used to say that Lyon is a good compromise between an active city and a good way of life. But I don't exclude to live elsewhere in the future.

Where can you find inspiring influences in France?

Museums, magazines, exhibitions, culture in general. But also the internet, like almost everyone today.

How would you define French creativity?

French graphic design is in my opinion very intellectualised like French culture. It involves the search of meaning, correlation with text and references.

What kind of creative practice would you consider unorthodox in the country?

Cheese making?

What do you plan to do next?

There are many things that I would like to explore in the future. Maybe more self-initiated projects and experimentations to find my own creative grammar.

01 / Wemotion, 2013. Visual identity and stationery for Wemotion, a motion design and broadcast studio. Original logo by Antoine Eckart.

02 / Interaction Mode, 2013. Visual identity, catalogue and signage for Biennale Internationale Design Saint-Étienne. Commissioned by Village des Créateurs.

03 / Festival des Musiques Innovatrices, 2014. Visual identity for the 22th edition of the music festival in Saint-Étienne. Co-created with Clément Le Tulle-Neyret.

02

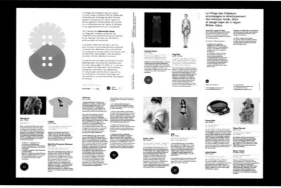

04 / Echo, 2015. Visual identity, catalogue and signage for a D'DAYS (Designers Days) event in Paris. Commissioned by Village des Créateurs.

05 / Excerpts, 2014. Excerpts from 2014 projects.

04

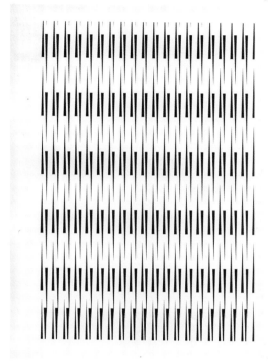

LO VOLUPTA, SPEREPERUM FUGIT,
ENE VIDE; CORIBUS DELENE VO;
LUPTIBUS PROR, MOSSEQUIS QUI,
IN CULPARUPTAE QUI UT; AUT IP-
SUM IPSUNT, SAM, SUM LIQUO
CONECTAE, NOBIS EXPLAM QUO-
SAND, ICIANDE, SCIPSAPERUM,
NUS, CONSEDL OSAMUS ET QUOI;
BERIBERNAM CON; REST EXPLCI,
PSANIAN, DITIAM QUE OMNIM; QUI
TIUS SUM DOLUPTA, AUT ISANDEL
MAIORE, LATIST; IATUS!
DEVRAIT-ON, DEMANDER.

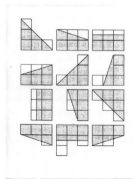

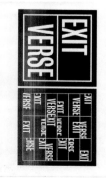

CRUSCHIFORM

Art direction, graphics, illustration
Paris

With great emphasis on colour coherence and geometric structure, CRUSCHIFORM's illustrations come as pure graphic poetry. Created and run by Marie-Laure Cruschi since 2007, CRUSCHIFORM has been favoured by fashion magazines, children's book publishers, as well as music and luxury brands that require imaginative presentations of complex and sometimes abstract subjects. The Paris-based creative studio's solutions are narrative, detailed and analytical, combining typography and graphic art. Portrait by Melania Avanzato.

01

Can you tell us something about your creations?

If I have to describe my universe with four adjectives, they will be 'dreamlike', 'copious', 'colourful' and 'geometric'.

How would you identify your artistic style with French culture?

The posters created around 1930 to 1950 as the French government started to promote tourism in France have significant impact on my art. Examples include the famous *Normandie* (1935) and the *Nord Express* (1927) illustrated by Cassandre. You will find these influences in my work, whether it's drawn for children (e.g. *À toute vitesse* published by Gallimard) or adults (see *Cabins* published by Taschen).

How do you usually get yourself ready to create?

I have a rather cerebral and methodical approach to my work. Starting with documentation allows me to return to the topics I'm not familiar with. A mood board helps me conceive a colourful atmosphere, an aesthetic universe. After that I do my sketch in black and white to develop a visual formula, and establish contrasts and line structures with initial colouring. At the end, I finalise my work on my computer. It has taken me great patience and determination to come this far.

What makes you come to work in France?

Living in Paris was a necessity for me to work as an illustrator. Paris (and France in a broad sense) has an exceptional dynamic in the field of children's book publishing. Our strong historical patrimony and practical knowledge in graphic design is our undeniable wealth, but French minds (rather divided) and traditions can be an obstacle to creation sometimes. Today I enjoy very much the freedom and flexibility my work nature gives me. I can work anywhere in the world as long as I have my work tools and internet access, and share my knowledge and affinities with my customers from Germany, Britain and Sweden. To me, opening up myself to the world is just as important as reconnecting with my own origin.

Where can you find inspiring influences in France?

I find my balance between my home town Cévennes, and Paris, for its energy, vibrant culture and countryside where I can recharge and meditate. My sensitivity to colour drives my work and my attention. It is what motivates me, support me emotionally and how I tell stories. In fact everything can be an inspiration. Contrasting colours and forms of design, fashion and architecture inspire me as much as the graphic rhythms and the play of light in nature. I'm particulary drawn to the work of Le Corbusier, Auguste Perret and Memphis.

What do you plan to do next?

I'm looking to combine my artistic practice with art direction on multidisciplinary projects that allow me to work across various disciplines of applied arts, whether it is to be done with artists, craftsmen or brands, particularly in the luxury sector. My wish is to bring different talents and creative energies into creative and ambitious projects.

— *Marie-laure Cruschi, Founder of CRUSCHIFORM*

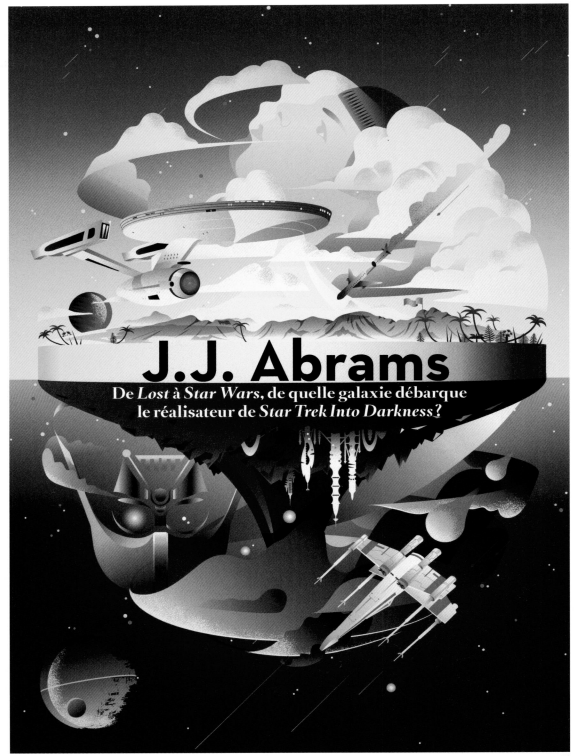

J.J. Abrams
De *Lost* à *Star Wars*, de quelle galaxie débarque le réalisateur de *Star Trek Into Darkness*?

02

02 / J.J. Abrams' Univers, 2013. Cover art for movie magazine Trois couleurs #111 about the anthologie of J.J Abrams to coincide its Cannes Film Festival screening in 2013.

03 / This New Noise, 2014. Cover art for a book that investigates the history, controversy and success of British broadcaster, BBC. Commissioned by publisher, Faber & Faber.

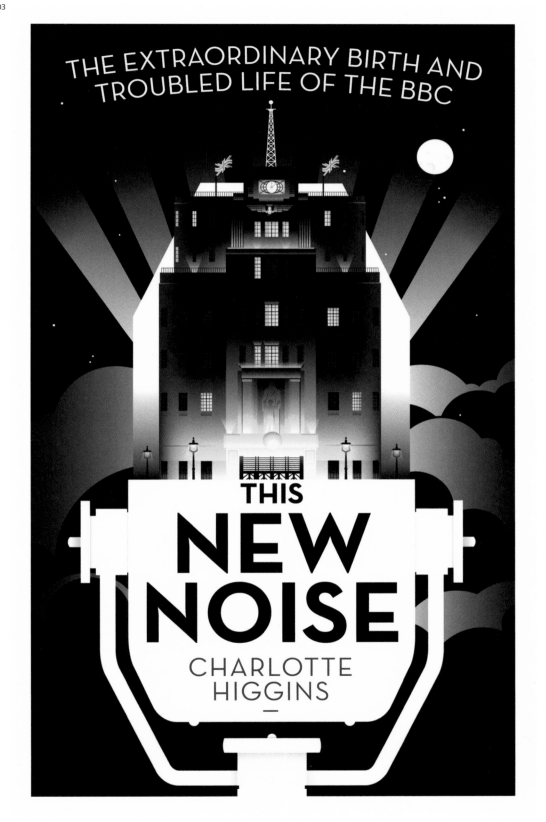

THE EXTRAORDINARY BIRTH AND TROUBLED LIFE OF THE BBC

THIS
NEW
NOISE

CHARLOTTE
HIGGINS
—

04 / Cabins, 2014. Illustrations
introduce contemporary cabins in
60 chapters for an architectural
book authored by Philip Jodidio and
published by Taschen..

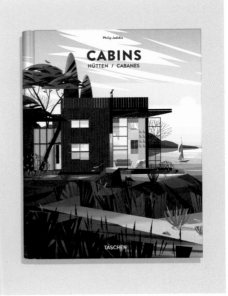

Enfant Terrible

Art direction, graphics
Grenoble

Enfant Terrible dreams up ambitious solutions the way their name suggests. Placing their focus on creative concepts and visual coherence, the agency works across wide-ranging mediums with a team of photographers, movie-makers, web designers and art directors to build smart graphic systems that connect visions and minds. Enfant Terrible is headed by creative director Nicolas Richard who was born in in the Rhône-Alpes region of southeastern France and has been practicing graphic design since the age of 16.

01

Can you tell us something about your creations?

Graphic design's current evolves quickly so we always try to push the limits by creating fresh and modern design. The psychology of colours and shapes are important to us.

How would you identify your artistic style with French culture?

We have graphic design and typography masters like Cassandre, who produced bold and neat graphic design where the purpose was as straightforward as the aesthetics. Similarly, we believe that the fewer elements a solution contain, the more powerful a design can be, given that the elements are chosen carefully.

How do you usually get yourself ready to create?

We run a blog (images.enfanterrible.fr) where we collect images that we like. It's been running for about five years now. Every day we explore the internet to feed it with photography, graphic design, animated gif, illustration, type and so on. There is no particular warm-up, I personally try to have my head filled with images 24/7. Also, I could say that music has given me a lot of energy through all this years.

What makes you stay in France?

There is a thought to establish a company abroad but we just love Grenoble. We live in one of the most beautiful part of France in my opinion, at the heart of French Alps near Italy and Switzerland. I'm just used to being surrounded by the mountains, it brings me peace and safeness.

Where can you find inspiring influences in France?

There are a lot of talented designers in France, especially in small, people-oriented studios. In Paris of course, but also in Lyon, Dijon, Crest, and many other cities. Some examples are Atelier Tout va bien, Helmo, Akatre, Les Graphiquants and Leslie David.

How would you define French creativity?

Maybe the sensitivity, with emotions and soul-reaching design. At least it is what I believe in.

What kind of creative practice would you consider unorthodox in the country?

As long as it gives birth to something interesting, there is no unorthodox way to experiment. Designs in the French music industry always surprises me. There is strong visual especially for festivals, club venues and record labels. They are often very contemporary, bold and neat, like the design we like to practice.

What do you plan to do next?

When the company starts to run on its own, I want to travel around the globe to meet new people and to work with them. China is really appealing. I'm planning to go to Hong Kong but I don't know when I'll have the opportunity.

01 / Too Cool For School, 2012-13. Posters for an electronic music event, with a wink at the kids who never fit in with traditional education. Photo by Léo Bigiaoui. Modelled by Rocco Di Pietro, Nancédy Keita.

02 / Studio Shots, 2012-15. Studio work.

*03 / Armistice, 2015. Art direction
and illustrations for three tracks
by electronic band Armistice,
namely North, Sonar and Mist.*

*04 / Bassodrome Festival 2015, 2015. Visual communication system
for the fifth edition of Bassodrome Festival to combined with visual
FX, VJing and movies produced by Stuffmaker, The Mad Studio, Live
FX and Larsen Color Production.*

Florent
Gomez

Art direction, graphics
Bordeaux / Amsterdam

With a penchant for typography and unconventional expressions, Florent Gomez applauds the sense of discipline and consistency proposed in Swiss and Dutch design through his designs. Having interned at Mainstudio (Amsterdam) and Maiarelli Studio (New York), this young French designer has built a portfolio comprised of cultural and design client works that cross the fields of branding, digital, editorial and interactive designs. Gomez' distinctive language emphasises concept which then he illustrates in between details.

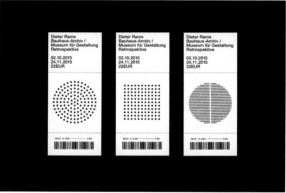

01 / Dieter Rams — Retrospektive, 2015. Branding proposal for the retrospective exhibition on Dieter Rams.

Can you tell us something about your creations?

I have always found European design inspiring, especially Swiss, Dutch and German designs, and I think it's something you see in my work. What I like about their design is their level of discipline and consistency in their creative process. I try to integrate this vision of design into sometimes a more contemporary approach. I'm also inspired by experimental approaches that reverse aesthetic codes to highlight strong concepts. I think it's more important to produce work that makes sense and not to fall into aesthetic trends that are often too fragile.

How would you identify your artistic style with French culture?

My style evolves. Even if the direction stays the same, I discover new things in every studio I work at, such as Maiarelli in New York or Mainstudio in the Netherlands, and from there I slowly build my own graphic language. I don't think that I can identify my style with the French culture but more with European culture, in reference to my graphic influences.

How do you usually get yourself ready to create?

I spend most of my free time catching what's new in the art and design world. I also spend a lot of time in books which is for me the best source of inspiration. The need to create to me is not a problem but rather a motivation. Design does not repeat. Every project is different and you can bring in totally unknown directions as you approach it.

What makes you stay in France?

France is a country steeped in history and its cultural wealth offers a huge playing field. It would be bad as graphic designer not to enjoy it. It is very important for me to stay connected with French culture. I try to travel a lot and working in France is a good way for me to share my experience.

Where can you find inspiring influences in France?

France is a really creative country on many levels. Visual art and French literature are the foundations of our visual culture today. This lay the foundation for the success of various fields such as cinema, music or design, and that makes us one of the most creative and culturally rich countries in the world.

What kind of creative practice would you consider unorthodox in the country?

I think that there is no such thing as "unorthodox" in creative practice. There's something unorthodox in each discipline and it is very important that it remains this way, that people are free to express themselves the way they want. Orthodox or not, creations must continue to evolve, to shock and enable open debates on our society and our way of thinking. Without that, creation has no meaning.

What do you plan to do next?

To start a studio in Bordeaux with my friend Thibaud Sabathier and teach in design schools to share my experiences to young creatives.

[UP AND GO un manifeste de l'art en action] UP AND GO!

02 / UP AND GO, 2014. Branding for the exhibition series that focuses on photography and jewellery design. Co-created with Thibaud Sabathier and Florent Marigo. Photo by Noellie Fournier. Commissioned by Chambre204.

03 / DUNK, 2015. Branding for DUNK, a photography, art and design exhibition at Abstract Galer, New York.

03

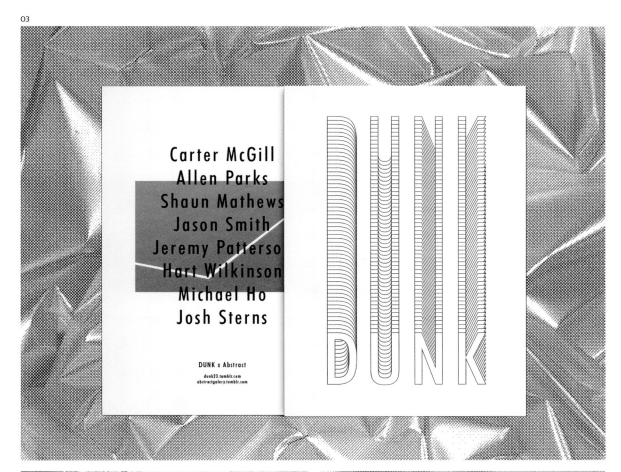

Florent
Tanet

Art direction, photography
Paris

Florent Tanet has the ability to turn ordinary scenes and objects into remarkable photographs. Refused to be bound by mediums, Tanet works at the intersection of art, sculpture, graphic design and photography, exploiting objects' materiality and connotations in unusual context. Since 2013, he devotes himself exclusively to photography and art direction with a strong interest for still-life. The French photographer and art director Florent Tanet (b. 1987) works and lives in Paris.

Can you tell us something about your creations?

I'm a multidisciplinary still life photographer working at the intersection of art, sculpture, graphic design and photography. My photos transform ordinary scenes and objects into something complex and remarkable. I enjoy the complete freedom of playing with these objects and using them as materials to create my compositions.

How would you identify your artistic style with French culture?

It's difficult to describe what is French culture today. The theme of my work is often oriented towards what constitutes the identity of the French culture — the art of living. I also have the chance to work with magazines and French companies such as Lacoste, Chanel and Le Bon Marché, whose history is steeped in French culture.

How do you usually get yourself ready to create?

I take photos everywhere with my iPhone, retrieve objects from the streets, take notes and do a lot of research on the internet (I'm from the tumblr generation) and in magazines. It's a routine that I always do before starting a new series.

What makes you stay in France?

This is where I grew up. I am very attached to the French culture. I also have my haunts and my professional network here.

Where can you find inspiring influences in France?

There are great cultural activities in France, especially in Paris where institutions are located and alternative projects flourish. Everything about France is so varied that we can find inspirations in all situations and particularly in our daily lives.

How would you define French creativity?

There is a multicultural blend of creativity in France and especially in Paris, with many foreigners coming to work in the city. The influences are multiple, with origins varying from the Mediterranean to Scandinavia. The French creativity comes from this melange and it is difficult to define it.

What kind of creative practice would you consider unorthodox in the country?

I don't think there is something more unorthodox than another in terms of creativity.

What do you plan to do next?

I have several personal projects in mind that I'd like to complete for a long time, especially about collage. I try to keep working on different artistic projects.

01 / *M LE MONDE, 2015. Editorial photography for M le Magazine du Monde that captures the work of six Parisian chefs with six salads.*

02 / *Le goût de, 2014-15. Editorial photography about tastes for Les Echos Magazine — Série Limitée.*

03 / *LIBERATION, 2014-15. Editorial photography for French newspaper Libération.*

02

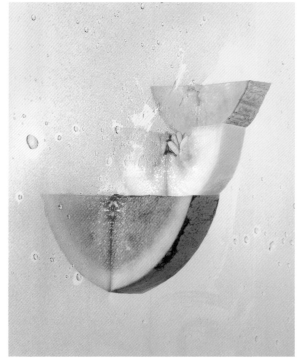

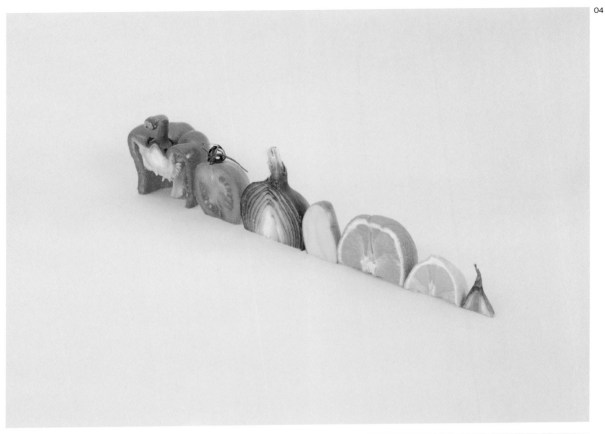

04 / *Colorful Winter, 2013. Photography for the exhibition held by department store La Grande Épicerie du Bon Marché.*

05-06 / *Daily Purism, 2014. Editorial photography for Un-titled Magazine.*

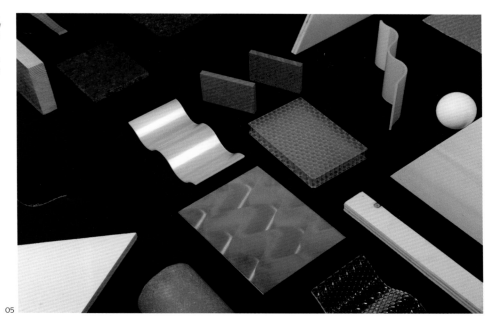

05

06

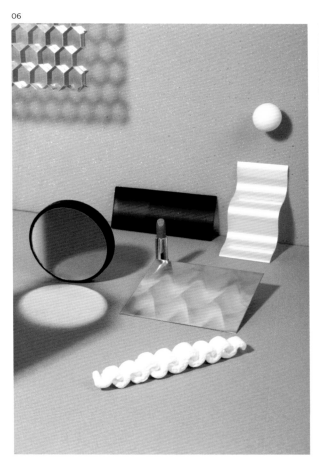

07

07 / *L'équilibre, 2015. Editorial photography for Causette magazine.*

FØLSOM
Studio

**Art direction, graphics,
furniture design**
Paris

Founded in 2012, Følsom is a trio of designers dedicated to providing all-medium solutions that combine scenography, graphics, fashion, interior and product designers. The Norwegian name "Følsom" sums up their creative attitude, indicating unique and coherent results that are delicate and meticulously executed. Their extensive network of specialists become part of their basic dynamic and versatility that enable the team to personalise projects of varied objectives and scales.

Can you tell us something about your creations?

Working together with our own design skills and with the same engagement on creative concepts allow us to find fresh ideas. Our work is defined by our need to give meaning to every project and to pay attention to details. Nothing is left to chance, each project is uniquely tailored to adapt to each request. And above all, we love what we do and we hope that it can be felt.

How would you identify your artistic style with French culture?

We live in Paris and this is an opportunity to encounter a wide range of different people and cultures. France is a country full of art and cultural history and our design practice is inspired by all of this. We are also marked by our lifestyle. We like that our inspirations are cosmopolitan and promote diversity in creativity.

How do you usually get yourself ready to create?

We start a project meeting around a table with coffee and croissants. We think and share our thoughts freely. One of us write everything down and we debate about the result. We then make visual experiments with a lot of materials. This important step is the best way to find a solid and original concept we are proud to submit to our clients.

What makes you stay in France?

When we first started we had an opportunity to settle in Paris and we seized it. Since then, we have developed a network of collaborators we enjoy working with. Although it is not always easy to deal with the little awareness about the values of graphic design in France, as shown again in recent government measures, it brings satisfaction when we can support our customers and lead them further than what they had imagined. We also are open to the chance of experiencing other countries in the future.

Where can you find inspiring influences in France?

Our inspirations mostly come from the exhibitions or live performing arts we can see here in Paris. They also come from our reading, everyday life and travels through the country.

How would you define French creativity?

We think French creativity is manifold due to the differences between designer generations, their creative process forged by studies and their clients. Although rich and dynamic, French creativity is sometimes slowed down by mimetism and the fear to dare. That said, we are confident. We see beautiful projects every day made by inspiring designers who never create forms to the detriment of the meaning.

What do you plan to do next?

To develop our own range of products and auto-edit our furniture designs. We also wish to design a collection of small objects, decoration items and graphic designs in order to create an online shop.

01 / Wedding invitation set, 2015.
Invitation and typography for
print workshop Imprimerie du
Marais's e-shop, La Belle Histoire.

01

02 / Archi Design Branding, 2014. Visual identity and stationery for the interior design studio, Archi Design.

03 / La Cicciolina restaurant matches, 2015. Matches packaging and illustration for Parisian restaurant, La Cicciolina.

02

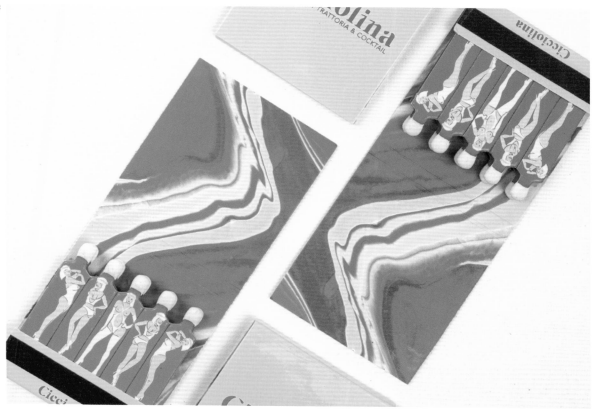

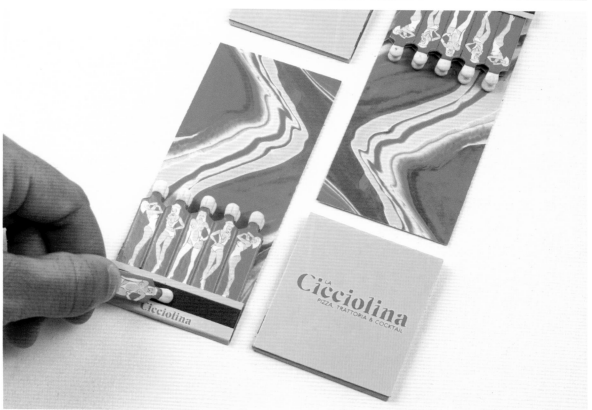

03

04 / *Creators and Craft Studios Show, 2014. Visual identity and event communication for the Creators and Craft Studios Show by Ateliers d'Art de France. Photos by photoproevent.*

05 / *Shabu Sha menu, 2014. Menu design for Shabu Sha, a Japanese restaurant in Paris.*

04

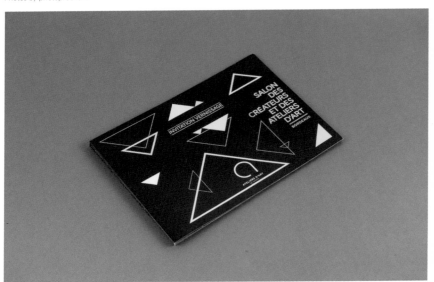

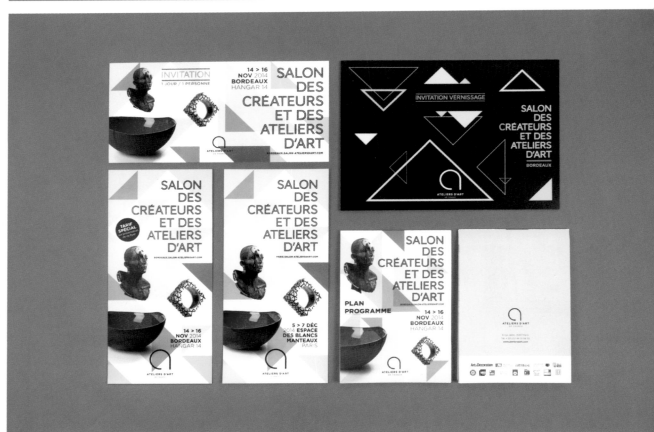

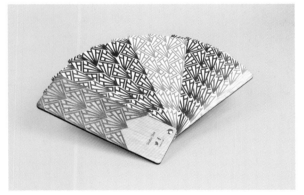

Giga Kobidze

Art direction
Paris

Giga Kobidze's work reflects the interplay between art, design, music, technology and traditional media. Keeping a balance between personal and client works, Kobidze lives his dream and passion for art and visualises life, people and memories through illustrations and typographic innovations. Professionally trained at Tbilisi State Academy of Arts, the Georgian-born designer and illustrator embraces changes and splits his energy and time between France, Georgian and the States.

Can you tell us something about your creations?

As I advance in finding new ways to express myself, I begin to understand more and more that my art is intimately linked to the duality and parallelism that reflects my personality, which I attempt to convey through my work.

How would you identify your artistic style with French culture?

French culture is unique. I believe it encompasses a much wider definition of culture than the one that is used elsewhere that confines our ability to express ourselves. French culture flourishes in an environment of expressive freedom that allows people to subconsciously mirror themselves and reflect on every action and movement in life. If my art permits me to transmit a portion of that sense of freedom, I have successfully done my job as an artist.

How do you usually get yourself ready to create?

It depends. I can be inspired by various inputs. Everyday life provides us with the particles that we can build on. They boil with emotions, which provide the foundation and structure that mark the starting point to build and express ideas. As an artist, having a blank canvas or screen is the greatest motivation to create.

What makes you come to France?

What can I say about Paris? It is just magnificent. Filled with history, art, emotion and challenges. It inspires every artist, no matter the medium, no matter where they come from.

Where can you find inspiring influences in France?

The aesthetic sense is deeply embedded in every corner of this country. The flow of life is communicated through its vibrant people, their energy, and their style as you travel through France. The movement of life here, with the innate sense of individuality is a constant inspiration for me. I love it!

How would you define French creativity?

French creativity comes from the roots. It comes from a rebellious spirit, an energy and a curiosity that is centuries old. I understand completely why the French have excelled at conveying emotions through different creative paths through art, be it graphic art, digital art, haute couture or its cuisine.

What do you plan to do next?

I don't like to plan for the future, rather I consider myself a gatherer of visual positives, of emotions and energy. Translating this creatively into my art is a form of exposure of my inner self. It is as exciting as any voyage of exploration that I can imagine.

01 / Anonymous, 2015. Digital art illustrations on the conflicts of the mind-body relationship.

02 / BEWARE of FALSE PROPHETS, 2012. Digital art illustrations on the four elements of life — earth, water, air and fire respectively.

03 / SEVEN – Diversities of Human
Behaviour, 2014. Digital art illustrations
that reflects seven diversities of human
behaviour and their effect on the state of
our soul and mind – Sin being the only
feature in common.

Grégoire Alexandre

Photography, scenography
Paris / New York

Born in Rouen in 1972 and schooled at the National School of Photography (ENSP) in Arles, Grégoire Alexandre is equal parts installation artist, illusionist, set designer and, as Christian Lacroix describes, poet. Cinema was his first interest, but he had switched to photography which he can more likely handle on his own. Alexandre's work has appeared in publications like Wallpaper, Vanity Fair and the world of Hermès, and Festival International of Fashion and Photography in Hyères, 2003. He has also collaborated with music artists such as Etienne Daho, Charlotte Gainsbourg, Yann Tiersen, and Yelle.

01

Can you tell us something about your creations?

I work mainly on commissioned studio photography. A large part of my projects is done before the shoot — finding ideas, collecting or creating the elements and discussing with the team if needed. My images are often a bit abstract and playful, using the photographic process as part of the composition to keep the ambiguity between reality and fiction.

How would you identify your artistic style with French culture?

There is something in the French culture and in my education (National School of Photography in Arles) that lead to asking myself questions about my medium and what is at stake when I'm creating an image — a sense of self-consciousness and a need to build on thinking.

How do you usually get yourself ready to create?

I have no routine. Every day is different. Every project is different and each of them dictates its own approach.

What makes you stay in France?

It's home. It's where I feel most comfortable. That's why I also like to work abroad. It's a bit more challenging with people of other backgrounds, other ways of working, new places, etc.

Where can you find inspiring influences in France?

Everywhere. Paris is filled with museums, concert venues, galleries… but the landscapes, the streets, the French way of life are also sources of inspiration.

How would you define French creativity?

I can't answer to that. One need to be out of it to analyse.

What kind of creative practice would you consider unorthodox in the country?

Nothing is forbidden.

What do you plan to do next?

I just want to carry on to explore new paths, be a bit less conceptual and more fragile — I'd like to avoid the stiffness that strong concepts can produce on images and try to let life in. I'll start with testing other types of light.

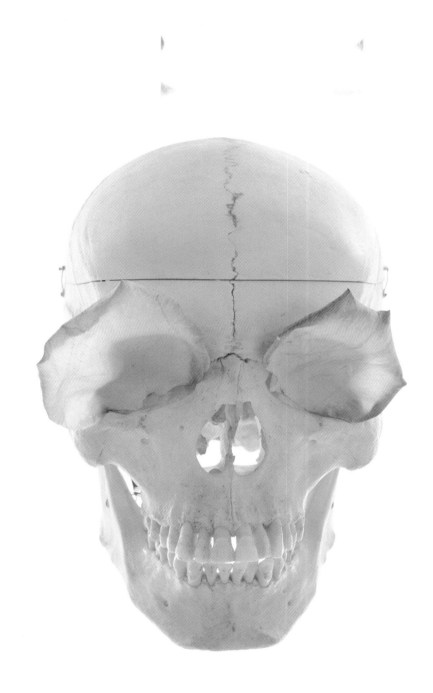

01 / Sleek magazine, 2010.
Fashion editorial for Sleek
Magazine. Styling by June Naka-
moto. Makeup & hair by Céline
Exbrayat. Modelling by Kathleen
Burbridge.

02 / Vanité, 2004.

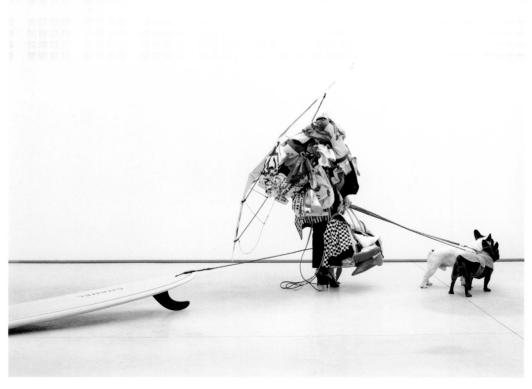

03

04 / Arjowiggins, 2009. Photography for the catalogue and website of Arjowiggins papers. Creative direction: Nicolas Champion, art direction: Frédéric Teysseire, set design: Hervé Sauvage, modelling: Stella Maxwell. Commissioned by Reflex agency.

04

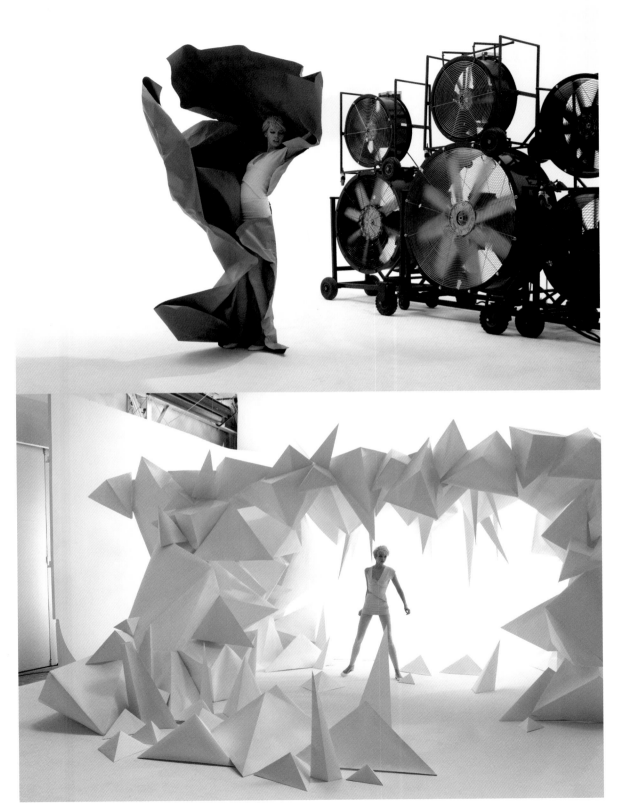

05 / Lily, 2007. Photography for Christian Lacroix pour La Redoute.

06 / Winter, 2012. Photography for Parmigiani magazine.

07 / Surrimpressions, 2011. Personal project. Makeup by Yacine Diallo. Modelling by Laia Bonastre.

In the pool

Art direction, graphics
Paris

Newly founded in 2015, In the pool leverages the creative synergies between ESAG Penninghen graduates Louise Harling and Géraldine Pace. When Harling's passion for clean vector forms and graphic patterns is matched with Pace's taste for photography and typography, the result is stark graphic work comprised of visual identities, editorial designs and print art. The duo's current portfolio features a range of collaborations, personal and client projects for cultural institutions and magazines.

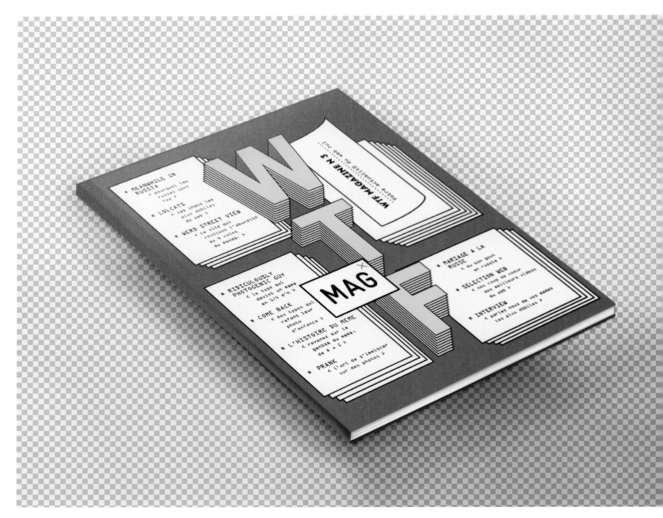

01 / WTF Magazine, 2015. Editorial design for a magazine that deals humorously with internet phenomena

Can you tell us something about your creations?

We both went to the same graphic school, ESAG Penninghen which was really elitist and traditional and it has been a hard sweat! We tried to free ourselves from these constraints while keeping the precious principles we learned in mind. We think this envy of lightness and expression is reflected in what we do and like a lot of people, we just want to live and have fun. We are still young! We experiment with what seems to be relevant without forgetting to use our sense of humour.

How would you identify your artistic style with French culture?

It's difficult to stand back from your work and the country you're living in. We both have a father of non-French descent (they are Swedish and Italian), so we have a cultural mix in our family which also reflects France in general. Perhaps the fact of being inspired by diverse influences is what brings us closer.

How do you usually get yourself ready to create?

For most of the time, we go out! We walk or sit on a terrace and have a major brainstorm. We come up with different ideas, clear them out until we agree on a really good one and completely immerse in it. But we never put ourselves under pressure!

What makes you stay in France?

Honestly, we were quite sure we would be living in another country, but we can't! We're extremely attached to this country. It is impossible to get bored by the omnipresent culture here. There are always new exhibitions, concerts or cool parties and this dynamic is really beneficial to our work.

Where can you find inspiring influences in France?

Everywhere! Paris is a city of endless inspiration! The street is a real means of expression in Paris. We are always pleasantly surprised when we see super funky posters promoting classical events. The amazing posters Pierre Jeanneau created for the Belleville Theatre is especially memorable. There are always something interesting to see and a lot of specialised libraries.

How would you define French creativity?

It seems cliché that France in the eyes of the world is all about luxury goods, traditions, good food…because France is also the result of anti-conformism as reflected in its art, fashion and the bolder graphic design that always try to differentiate itself from other European design. Situated in the middle of western Europe, our borders are quite open to ongoing immigration. In a way, we lose a bit of our "national identity" (not like Switzerland for example), but on the other hand it creates emulation and makes France a rich cultural crossroad.

What do you plan to do next?

Artistic direction for video clips could be really interesting! We'd like to create patterns and designs for fashion too. We're also planning a trip to Japan. In the future, we'd love to expand our team, work with different people and have a new premises with a big swimming pool!

C = 0% M = 55% J = 30% N = 0%   C = 60% M = 0% J = 0% N = 0%   C = 0% M = 0% J = 100% N = 0%   C = 0% M = 0% J = 0% N = 0%

Bernino Sans Condensed regular

ABCDEFGHIJKLMNOPQRSTUVWXYZ
abcdefghijklmnopqrstuvwxyz

Bernino Sans Condensed semi-bold

ABCDEFGHIJKLMNOPQRSTUVWXYZ
abcdefghijklmnopqrstuvwxyz

Hello ! We are Louise Harling and Géraldine Pace, two graphic designers from Paris (and around...). We are very dynamic, maybe too much, but the good news is that all this energy is reflected in our work. This is why we decided to open a studio called "In the Pool" specialized in visual identity and print but also in chill evenings by the water. If we write you today it is because we loved your work ! So feel free to contact us if you are interested in working with us, swimming with us or just meeting over for coffee.

In the pool studio

Géraldine Pace & Louise Harling

+33 (6) 45 79 86 08

inthepool fr

hello@inthepool fr

180 bd Richard Lenoir 75011 Paris

Hello ! We are Louise Harling and Géraldine Pace, two graphic designers from Paris (and around...). We are very dynamic, maybe too much, but the good news is that all this energy is reflected in our work. This is why we decided to open a studio called " In the Pool" specialized in visual identity and print but also in chill evenings by the water. If we write you today it is because we loved your work! So feel free to contact us if you are interested in working with us, swimming with us or just meeting over for coffee.

02 / In the pool Visual Identity,
2015. Photo by Florian Chaudat.

03

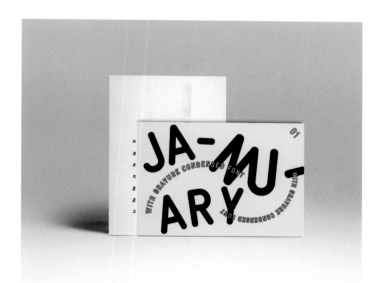

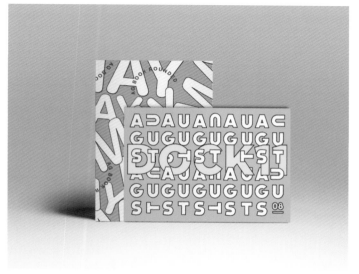

03 / One month / One font, 2015.
Typographic calendar presents
one different font every month.

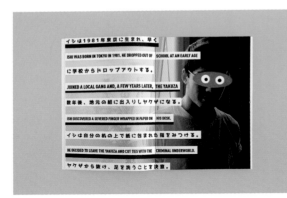

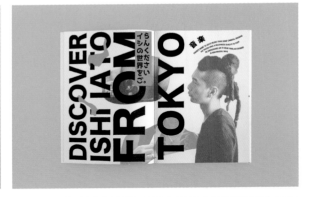

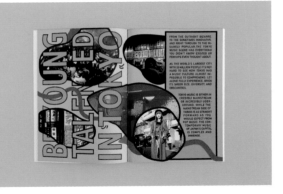

04 / Dj Set Editorial, 2015. Editorial design.

05 / Paris Climat, 2015. Self-initiated posters for one of the biggest international conference on global warming.

Jeff Pag

Art direction, graphics
Paris

Jefferson Paganel is a graphic designer and art director based in Paris. Graduating EPSAA in 2010 with a Master's degree in graphic design under his belt, Paganel began his career working at some of Paris' most prominent studios, such as Leslie David and Sid Lee Paris. Past work encompasses visual branding, type design and editorial design for clients ranging from fashion brands to creative individuals. Paganel is currently an art director at design agency LaPetiteGrosse.

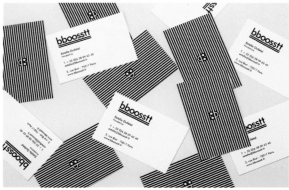

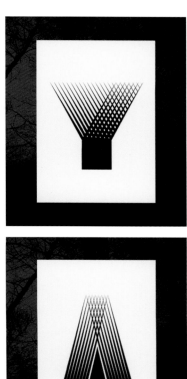

01 / *BBOOSSTT Visual Identity, 2014. Logo, corporate stationery and website for a new human resource consulting company, created at LaPetiteGrosse.*

02 / *Double, 2010. Type design for Double Magazine, created at Leslie David.*

02

Can you tell us something about your creations?

My creations are often bold and minimalist, sometimes with a slight touch of fun through words or colours. I like to work for big companies as well as small shops that deal with food, luxury goods, fashion, spirits and liquors…I design with passion. I'm always excited to start a new project to learn new things and find the best idea. It's important for me to pass on the pleasure to people who see and touch my work.

How would you identify your artistic style with French culture?

I am not sure I have an artistic style other than starting with a strong and meaningful idea. Besides, connecting to the world through the internet has prompted us to mix our styles with foreign influences. It's hard to define French culture today. I love Le Corbusier, all the modern movements in 1920s and Art Deco from its rich heritage, but I am also interested in designs from Scandinavia, United Kingdom, Germany, Japan, and always happy to discover new creations overseas.

How do you usually get yourself ready to create?

I often start by creating a long list of words on my notebook as a brainstorm exercise. I also do sketches inspired by book and internet references. I collect stuff I appreciate in folders on my laptop and boxes on my desk, they are very useful.

What makes you stay in France?

I was born and raised in France. I love this country and enjoy my life in Paris. This beautiful city has so many different sides and it always transforms. I like the dynamic! I travel a lot and I miss Paris every time.

Where can you find inspiring influences in France?

E-v-e-r-y-w-h-e-r-e! Books, movies, architecture, nature, friends, walking in the street, blogs, exhibitions, talks…

How would you define French creativity?

It's hard to talk about uniqueness of French creativity amidst global influences. Nice creations emerges every day around the world. But I want to point out that unfortunately in France we have clear boundaries between commercial, cultural and art projects, I don't know why, but it's hard to crossover!

What kind of creative practice would you consider unorthodox in the country?

Street art has become prominent and comes with very high creative quality. JR, Akroe, Space Invader, Remed…I think we also like to tackle sexual and provocative topics!

What do you plan to do next?

I would love to go further to bridge graphic design and fine art, to build and exhibit a project on a global scale, or create my own brand.

03 / Rebranding Atelier Herbez Architectes, 2015. Logo, corporate stationery, website design and portfolio book design for an architectural design agency in Paris.

04 / Pain Pain Visual Identity, 2015. Branding, corporate stationery and packaging for a new barkery, created at LaPetiteGrosse.

03

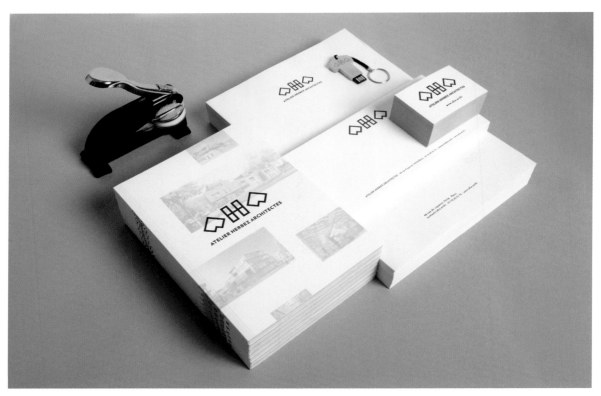

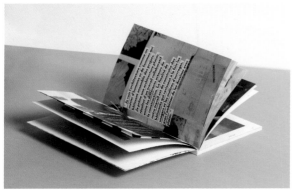

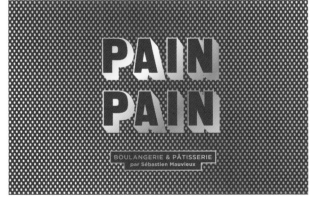

05 / ESMOD, 2011. Art direction
and editorial design for fashion
design institute ESMOD, created
in hands with François Prost at
Icône Paris.

06 / HYES branding, 2013. Copo-
rate stationery, poster and look-
book design for Parisian fashion
and jewellery label, HYES.

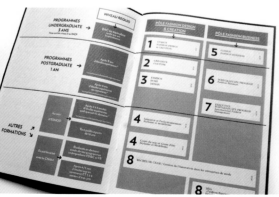

Jonas Sellami aka Sella

Graphics
Nantes / Los Angeles

Sella is the professional name of Jonas Sellami, who passes on his devout love for electronic music into his graphic design. From commissioned album artwork to personal work, Sella approaches each project with a strong desire to manipulate shapes and test production techniques that combine 3d renderings and manual methods. Besides his design pursuits, Sella is also part of French webzine, *Input Selector*, and a DJ and music producer under the alias Jonas Sella.

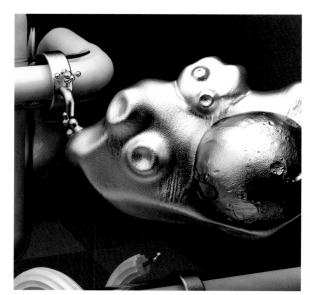

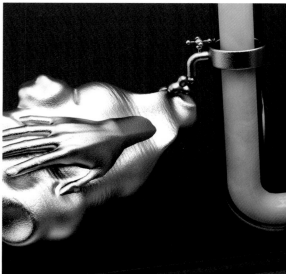

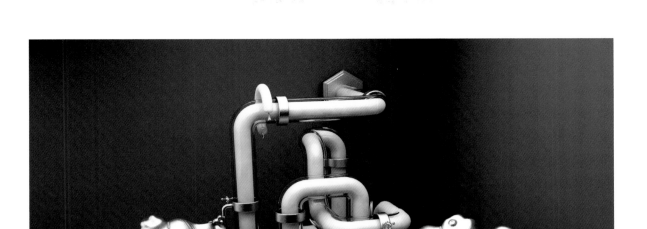

01 / *Alf Pipe, 2013. Personal experiment with renderings of pipes and shaders.*

Can you tell us something about your creations?

Born and raised in Nantes, France, I always officiate at multiple creative areas with pleasure. I enjoy playing with shapes and constantly try to blur boundaries between real life and the digital environment. Parallel to it, I also maintain a close relationship with music and try to participate as much as possible in the field.

How would you identify your artistic style with French culture?

Maybe I eat better cheese during my creative process? Haha! I couldn't tell. In fact, I try to take advantage of every culture, but it's always interesting to work on more traditional projects like wine packaging. I would have stumbled across design without being involved in music. At a point when you need to promote your events or your materials you start thinking about the visuals, which is really stimulating.

How do you usually get yourself ready to create?

I wake up at 5:30 in the morning for my daily cricket hunting base jump… just kidding! I don't have any routine way to live. My desk can be anywhere. But breakfast is important.

What makes you stay in France?

I am currently in California as some great opportunities arose. Nothing makes me stay at one place but a lot of things can draw me back to France.

Where can you find inspiring influences in France?

Obviously in Nantes. It's a super fun, creative and lively city. A must-visit destination for many. A lot of inspiring things are happening there. Each year there is this big creative event called Le Voyage à Nantes, which showcases lot of crazy architectural and artistic works. The city also hosts the Type Directors Club every year.

How would you define French creativity?

It's not better than any others, but is definitely one of its kind. I think French creativity has its very pronounced and committed side. It tries to make people think and react, and always delivers a strong message. The use of words and symbols really has always been an important part of it.

What kind of creative practice would you consider unorthodox in the country?

I've always been very attached to Georges Rousse's work. His sensitivity to composition and spatial arrangements make his productions unique.

What do you plan to do next?

I'm going to explore California!

*02 / Input Selector Campaign,
2013-15. Posters and flyers
promotes parties organised by a
French music webzine.*

*03 / Timid Records, 2012. Art
direction for a French electronic
music label.*

02

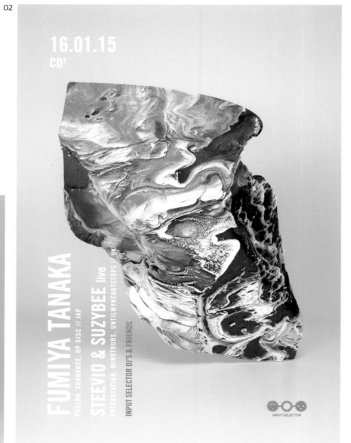

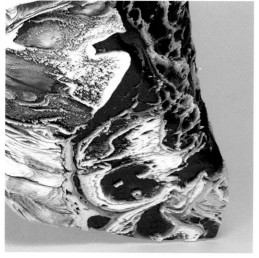

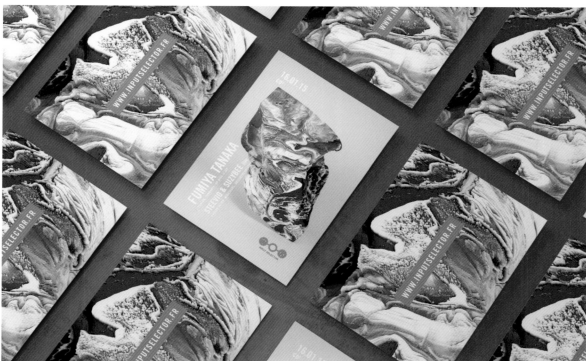

03

04 / Fluxe, 2013. Personal experiment with fluid behavior, shader and patterns.

05 / Input Selector Five Years, 2013. Flyers artwork celebrates the French music webzine's fifth birthday.

04

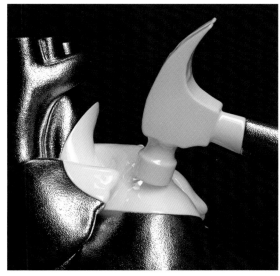

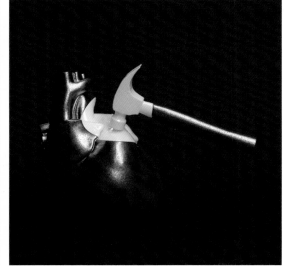

Julien
Lelièvre

Graphics, photography
Paris

Born in Rouen in 1979, Julien Lelièvre has been trained at ESAA Dupér-ré and ENSAAMA Olivier de Serres. In practice since 2004, Lelièvre had designed for Centre Pompidou, CNC, the Louvre, the departmental council of Department 93, etc. under the artistic direction of the late Erasmus Prize-winner Pierre Bernard at L'Atelier de Création Graphique, before setting up his own studio in 2010. He's also part of the Atelier collectif which he founded with a team of designers specialising in typeface and web design.

LE PEINTRE
ET SON MODÈLE
12 juin — 14 sept
MUSÉE
PICASSO
PARIS

www.
musee-
picasso
.fr

ANDRÉ VILLERS
CHEZ PICASSO
MUSÉE
PICASSO
PARIS

12.06.2013
18.07.2013

01

*01 / MUSÉE PICASSO PARIS, 2013. Proposed
logotype, visual identity and event communication
for The Picasso Museum of Paris. Co-created with
Emmanuel Labard and Jean-Baptiste Levée.*

Can you tell us something about your creations?

"De la grosse typo (just big typefaces)" as the Building Paris team says. Seriously, I am just trying to produce efficient designs that fully communicate the intentions of the client. Creativity in graphic design comes with specifications — the directions and recommendations client give us for the project. No good specification, no good design.

How would you identify your artistic style with French culture?

I don't really believe that young French graphic designers can be identified with a 'typical' French culture. French visual culture comes from advertising, not really from graphic design. Maybe the most interesting heritage is typography, in which designers such as Roger Excoffon excelled at a very open-minded way of work and a multidisciplinary approach.

How do you usually get yourself ready to create?

I start with internet routines before I work: websites, tumblrs and emails. I always have a notebook on my desk with a to-do list and notes for later.

What makes you stay in France?

Family, friends and the particularity of Normandy landscapes (and good wine).

Where can you find inspiring influences in France?

Here at L'Atelier collectif!

How would you define French creativity?

To believe that good design is for everybody. Not just for cultural places and cultivated people.

What kind of creative practice would you consider unorthodox in the country?

I don't know if we could consider it unorthodox but poster design for French cinema is really calamitous. France is not alone on the topic, unfortunately.

What do you plan to do next?

I have been practising photography solemnly since 2006. This year, in 2015, I have just done a series of photographs about "highway art" in France which involved five years of research, photo-taking and travelling. My next goal is to find an editor and publish a book with this work. Otherwise, I will be further practising photography in different fields: at someone's command or as my personal research.

LE MUSÉE PICASSO PARIS VOUS SOUHAITE LA BIENVENUE

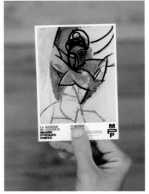

01

02

02 / ORKADRE, 2008-2012. *Book design for Orkadre Vol. 1-3, namely Lksir, Fabrice Houdry and Popay. Published by Piktur Éditions.*

03 / DESSANCE, 2013. *Logo, menu and business card for Dessance, a dessert bar in Paris. Concept by Philippe Baranes.*

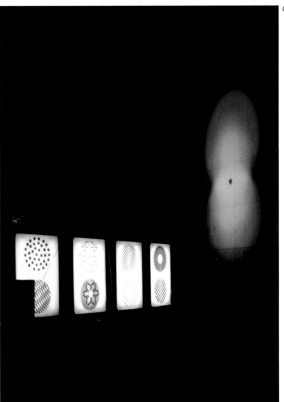

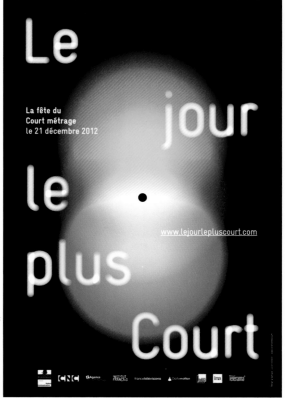

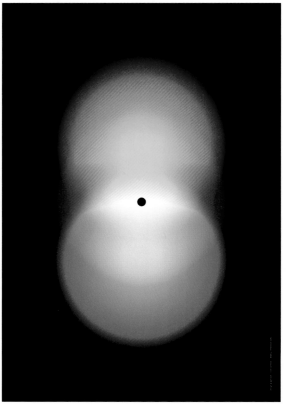

04 / LE JOUR LE PLUS COURT, 2012. Visual identity and poster for Le jour le plus court (The Shortest Day), a short film festival in France. Commissioned by CNC.

05

05 / MENS ALORS!, 2013-14. Visual identity and event communication for MENS ALORS!, a music and art festival in Mens, France. Edition 2013 illustration by Lison de Ridder / HSH crew.

Justine
Thouvenin

Art direction, photography
Paris

Born in Rouen and graduating from ESAG Penninghen in 2015 with a Master's degree in art direction, Justine Thouvenin has served several internships at French agencies before practising independently. These agencies include specialist magazine publisher Barrel Collection, as well as consultancies Brandelet+Devineau and Chic Paris, and from these experiences she honed her art direction, photo retouching and editorial design skills. Thouvenin's enthusiasm for fashion photography, graphics and typography is transparent in her work.

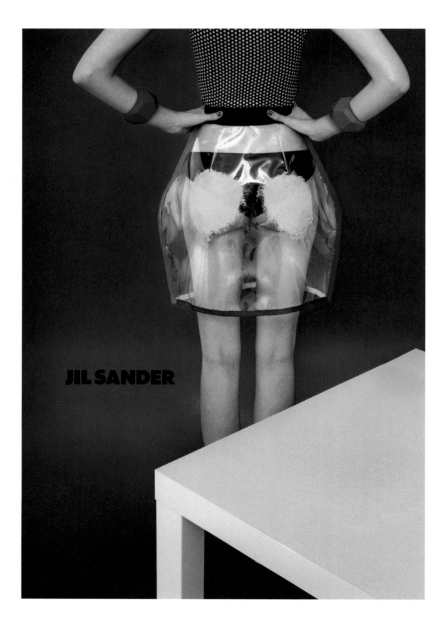

JIL SANDER

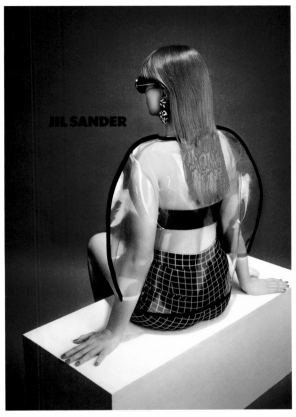

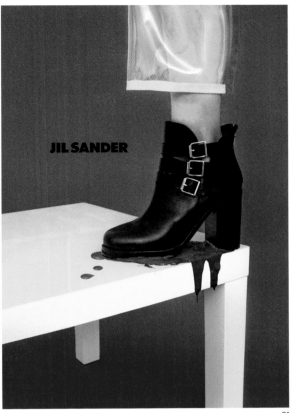

01 / Fresh Paint!, 2014. Fashion photography around the theme of fresh paint. Fashion design by Pierre Parent.

02 / Fauve Magazine, 2015. Art direction, photography and digital art for the Fauve Magazine editorial. Fashion design by Waki Huang, Pierre Parent and Joey Viet Nguyen. Makeup & Hair by Nolwenn Bechu, Sefedine Alaoui, Jingtong and Amélie Baraké.

Can you tell us something about your creations?

I think my creations are optimistic, sometimes offbeat. I try to find fun angles, play with colours, forms or details and to take retrospect on specific subjects.

How would you identify your artistic style with French culture?

I do not feel restricted by any school of thought. I feel free to try anything with aesthetics in mind. Everything is justifiable.

What makes you stay in France?

I love France, I love Paris, its freshness, café terraces and the many museums. I have my brand and my rituals. But I am not against leaving the country for a while to get in touch with other cultures. It is always rewarding to go beyond borders and I intend to do so soon. But France is still my home and I will always come back!

Where can you find inspiring influences in France?

French creativity can be found everywhere, in museums, exhibitions and libraries. Sometimes it may just be a scene in the subway, in the street, or the words of someone, sometimes it is the international creations that unconsciously revisit the "French touch"! I spent my day walking around Paris a few weeks ago, sitting alone for hours to watch others, to think, to lose myself somewhere in my head. I had the impression of being a foreigner among foreigners who keeps marvelling at the things right in front of my eyes. It's a crazy experience and opens my mind to new ideas!

How would you define French creativity?

Always with style and a great freedom of expression! France, like other countries, has a rich cultural and artistic past, how can it not inspire?! Our history of art and culture has offered as much freedom as the opportunities it creates.

What kind of creative practice would you consider unorthodox in the country?

Can we consider it as not responding to the rules accordingly? For me, it must bring the audience to think or to feel, regardless of what the feeling is. Picasso for example, has turned the principles of perception completely upside down with cubism. By transposing his thoughts into paintings, he managed to explain that the emotions distort one's vision of a person or of an act. He broke existing principles to assert his own vision.

What do you plan to do next?

I am full of ideas about fusing fashion photography with digital art. My problem is that I would like to do everything! So I will leave my future in the hands of fate and encounters that await me.

Klar

Art direction, graphics
Lyon / Paris

Before Klar was put in place in 2008, the creative team behind the agency has already been exploring visual culture and experiences through their publishing project, Kiblind Magazine. Launched in 2004, the quarterly's design, fashion and music content has won over a national audience to follow its updates. While Kiblind keeps running, Klar extends their design and publishing expertise to offer branding advice, art direction and communication design for ad campaigns and cultural clients.

01 / Bibliothèques de Paris, 2015. Poster campaign based on the theme "Culture sur place à emporter (Culture on the spot or to take away)".

Can you tell us something about your creations?

Klar was founded in 2008 by the team behind Kiblind Magazine. As the magazine's very own 'print atelier', the creative work of the two is closely connected. While having our own creative team, we're taking our projects to another level by collaborating with different French and foreign artists from the graphic design and communication fields.

How would you identify your artistic style with French culture?

Our work is modelled on our dear country! France is at the crossroads of different cultures and arts thanks to international trades and its easy accessibility. They all helped shape our country through age and we can still feel this multicultural heritage today. Our style is a perfect blend of the spontaneous and full-of-life Latin mind, the playful and understandable Anglo-saxon spirit and a meticulous and simple Nordic soul.

How do you usually get yourself ready to create?

Exchanging views with the team, digging deep into our books and the internet infinity, exchanging views with the team, defining a valid line of work, exchanging views with the team, approving ideas, exchanging views with the team, calling all of it into question, exchanging views with the team, et cetera.

What makes you stay in France?

Both Kiblind magazine and Klar are closely connected to where they are located. Our 'printed atelier' is a project born in a specific area called Lyon and shaped with specific people. We run our studios in Paris and Lyon for the same reasons. We like to work in connection with the people and structures that make the cities alive.

Where can you find inspiring influences in France?

Kind of everywhere. We're lucky to have a distinctive French culture marked by rich heritage and a flourishing contemporary creative scene. We know there will always be new things to look at and talented people to work with because of its multicultural background.

How would you define French creativity?

It's kind of like Zinedine Zidane's "Roulette" in soccer.

What do you plan to do next?

We hope we'll take the magazine as far as possible. It has been an amazing opportunity for us to explore the contemporary creative scene — especially in visual arts — a little bit further every day through this platform. The magazine also allows us to face the world of media in a fun and collective way.

02 / Kiblind #52 Spring Issue, 2015. Magazine cover co-created with Atelier Tout va bien connects issue number 52 to chess games. Detachable chess pieces inclusive.

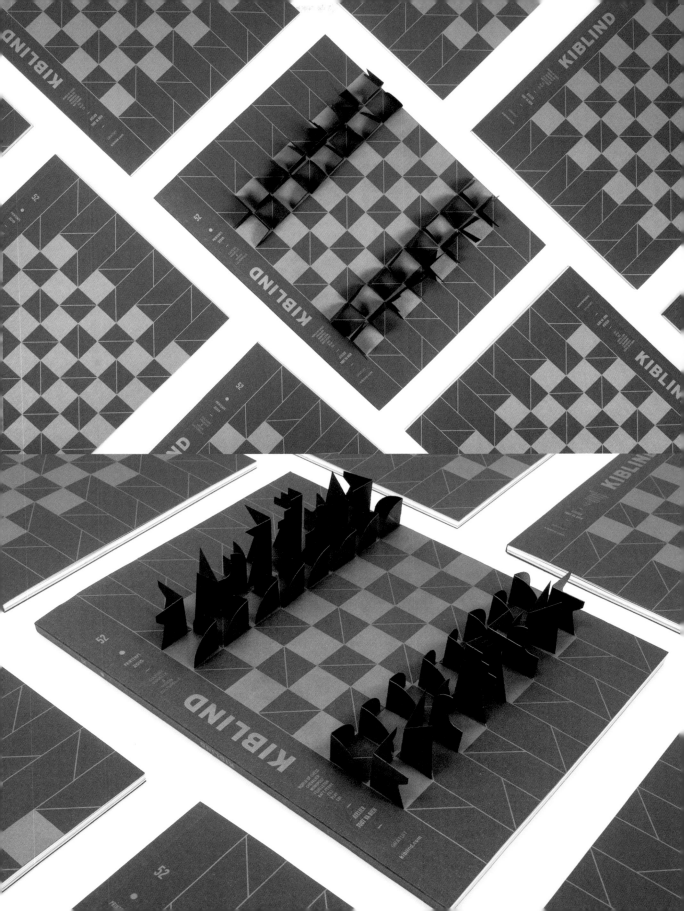

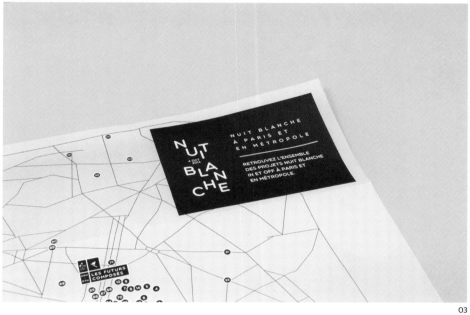

02

03 / Nuit Blanche, 2014. Programme design for the 13th Nuit Blanche artistically directed by José Manuel Gonçalves.

Les produits de l'épicerie

Art direction, graphics
Lille

Created by Philippe Delforge and Jérôme Grimbert in 2003, with Marieke Offroy joining in 2011. Les produits de l'épicerie aspires to excite people's imagination with their graphic and photographic images. To this end, they collaborate with photographers, artists, videographers, web designers and printers. The creative trio produces work in the fields of arts, commerce, music and architecture, with particular attention to creating powerful visual sensations and touches in the end results.

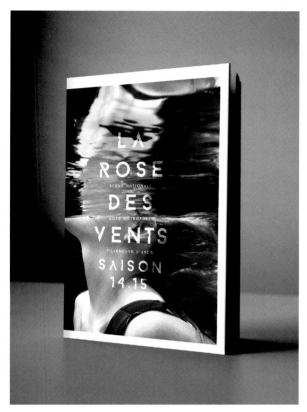

*01 / La rose des vents, 2014.
Visual identity and communication for the theatre La rose des
vents' season 14/15. Photo by
Ludovic Florent.*

Can you tell us something about your creations?

We work to desire and are always trying to renew our work. Our creations are designed for free interpretation but we do leave clues to help viewers understand them, and sometimes it's only after seeing the show or the exhibition that you are able to understand the design. But is it really important to understand the meaning of a poster? Above all, we want viewers to take ownership of what they see and interpret in their own way. It's also very important for us to get to know and meet our clients. We like to work in collaboration, talk and exchange ideas with them. We are not fans of the Powerpoint briefs sent by e-mail with a price list attached.

How would you identify your artistic style with French culture?

Each project is different, as is the client and event, but we do have a certain way of doing things. Let's say it's a dialogue between substance and form. Respectfully, our design is like a window that leads the public to discover the artists we work for. We like to extend this dialogue from the drawing on paper, to the forms, colours and even to the printer. We like to believe that, in our small way, we participate in the cultural life. French design is among our diverse influences, with the likes of graphic artist collective Grapus and studio Les Graphiquants affecting our graphic design approach in France.

How do you usually get yourself ready to create?

To begin with, and probably the most important thing after coffee is the music. We cannot work without it. We usually start with drawing, which guides us both onto creating the design in graphic composition. We work further to build, modify and refine once it is computerised.

What makes you stay in France?

We are born here and our families live here. We aren't that adventurous. Besides, the north of France, where we live, is very close to Belgium, the Netherlands, England and even Germany. We love our business trips though!

Where can you find inspiring influences in France?

We find inspirations all around us in people we meet and in our differences. But inspiration is not limited to France or even to graphics, anything can trigger an idea.

How would you define French creativity?

Rich, committed, diverse and courageous.

What kind of creative practice would you consider unorthodox in the country?

We believe that any form of creativity should be unorthodox.

What do you plan to do next?

Digital, engraving, serigraphy, video and all at the same time. Every field is interesting to explore.

02 / Ces architectures qui nous emballent, 2015. Exhibition invitation and poster for the exhibition Ces architectures qui nous emballent. Commissioned by Lille Architecture Center (MAV·NPDC).

03 / Bob, 2013. Logo and visual identity for Bob, a food truck by artist Erwin Wurm. Commissioned by Artconnexion and SPL Euralille.

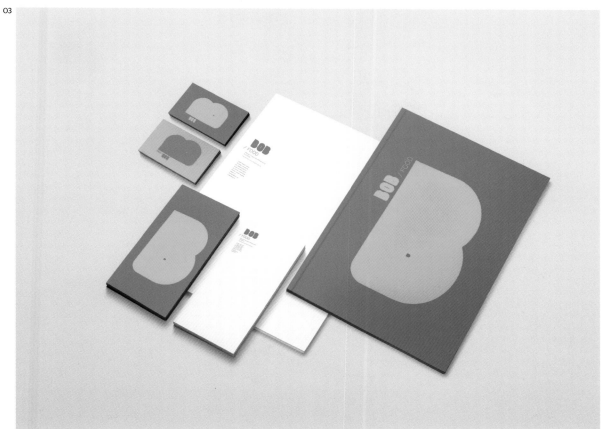

04 / *Le vivat, 2014. Visual identity and communication for the theatre Le vivat's season 14/15. Photo by Charly Desoubry.*

05 / *La rose des vents, 2015. Visual identity and communication for the theatre La rose des vents' season 15/16. Photo by Greg Verhaeghe.*

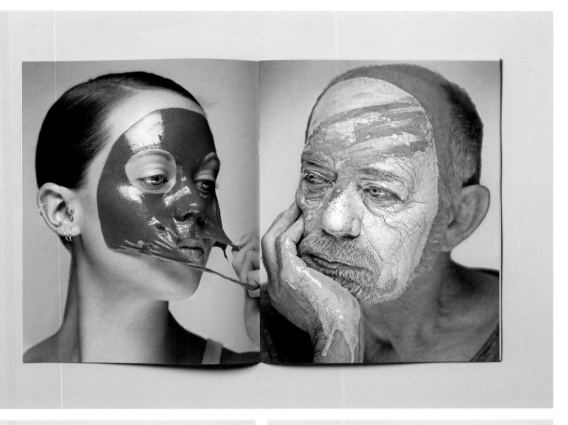

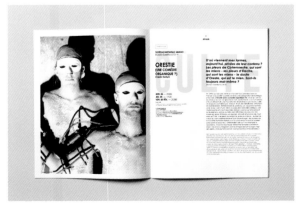

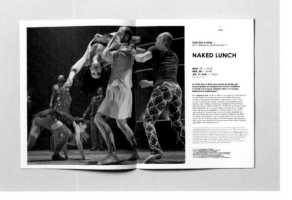

Lili des Bellons

Graphics, illustration
Clermont-Ferrand / Paris

Often outlandish, characterised by clashing fluoro colours and bold line work, Lili des Bellons' illustrations ooze a strange aura that blends imagination and memories. Her illustration themes vary from realistic architectural imagery to geometric figures and humanoid creatures, with a deep focus on colour, tone and texture. Lili des Bellons is the pseudonym of graphic designer Laurent Meriaux, who also dabbles in animation and web design. Lili des Bellons' work has appeared in Esquire Russia and German magazine Hohe Luft.

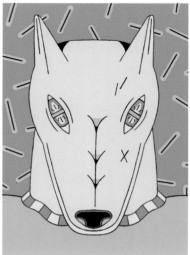

Can you tell us something about your creations?

I hope my work stimulates people. If creativity is a language, I hope to express myself as simply and clearly as possible.

How would you identify your artistic style with French culture?

There are diverse landscapes and different colours in France, which are very inspiring. I have a small crush on Provence's lavender fields and the colours of Canal du Midi. Regions like Brittany, Auvergne and the Camargue all have a unique ambiance. Perhaps these are reflected in my work. But what's most interesting for me is the diversity and cultures that my work represents. They feed my work.

How do you usually get yourself ready to create?

I think repetition is necessary to develop a technique. But technique is only a tool. The rest of the creative process is stimulated by the unexpected. I try to see, read, go out and travel as much as possible. My habit is that I especially like to draw at night (without really knowing why).

What makes you stay in France?

I love life here. I have travelled and seen wonderful things. But my roots are here.

Where can you find inspiring influences in France?

There are many architecture, museums and exhibitions in France. But if you come here, do not hesitate to seek and explore bizarre and unusual places. Browse the countryside and smaller towns. Each town has its own custom, landscapes and architecture.

How would you define creativity French?

I think creativity in France comes from cultural diversity.

What kind of creative practice would you consider unorthodox in the country?

In art schools here, there are still courses on colours (learning about decomposition and interaction) as well as on anatomy and modelling. I think it is as important to keep, learn and, if possible, understand these techniques as it is to forget them, breaking away from the standards and trying other things. Also, there are many disciplines and artists that demonstrate originality in the fields of fashion, architecture, animation, film and the arts in general. I had the opportunity to watch some very crazy short film productions in my school, namely *Camera Obscura* (2007, vimeo.com/24409767), *Yenkee Gal* (2008, vimeo. com/3173246) and *Tim Tom* (2002, vimeo.com/10766668).

What do you plan to do next?

For now I will continue to offer my work in the existing way. But I would also like to work on 2D and 3D animation. I took my time to learn the techniques of this craft.

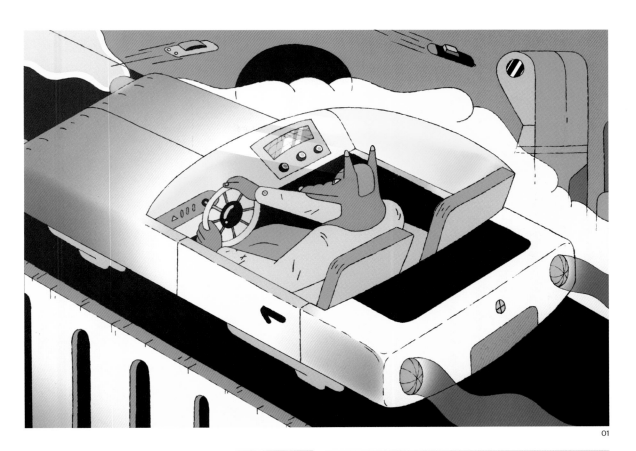

BELLONS

01 / Neon, 2015. A series of personal illustrations to experiment
on graphical representations and
colour associations.

02 / Blue, 2015.

02

Marc Da Cunha Lopes

Photography, post-production
Paris

Born in 1979, Marc Da Cunha Lopes studied photography in Gobelins Paris and graduated in 2005. Full of surreal references, his photographic imagery is the perfect union of his post-production wizardry and scientific knowledge in the sphere of biology. It is this interesting personal vocabulary that has later led to striking editorial commissions and ad campaigns for international brands such as Nike, Fiat, Peugeot and Sony PlayStation. His personal work "Vertebrata" was put up for public view for the first time at Galerie Rabouan Moussion, Paris, in 2011.

Can you tell us something about your creations?

I mainly do photography, photography post-production and props. I am known for my surrealistic works. I am based in Paris, but I work for advertising agencies from around the world. Some of my work has been exhibited in Parisian galleries.

How do you usually get yourself ready to create?

I usually start a project outside of my studio, in a café, a park or somewhere else outdoor, writing and drawing ideas on my notebook. I also listen to music when I draw my sketches. It helps me focus on my ideas.

What makes you stay in France?

I was born in France to Portuguese parents who fled from dictatorship in 1968. I grew up in Parisian suburbs before moving into the city when I started working and had enough money to pay for a small apartment. Then I could not really leave the city. It is where my friends, my family and my professional network are.

Where can you find inspiring influences in France?

I often go to exhibitions in Paris. There are a lot of venues where you can see great things. Even though international creations can be seen online, I prefer the real thing. I really like La Maison Rouge, a private foundation created by Antoine de Galbert, and also La Maison Européenne de la Photographie.

How would you define French creativity?

That's really hard to define because even if we have a great art legacy and tradition in France, most French people and artists are of foreign descent. All these cultures are melted to create something new. We also have good art schools which give us good education and techniques.

What kind of creative practice would you consider unorthodox in the country?

I think we are quite orthodox.

What do you plan to do next?

I always want to do films. I started on commercials last year. But I really want to go ahead and produce more personal work in the form of video. I also like indie video games and interactive storytelling (I played *Her Story* last month and it's really great!). I think there are a lot of possibilities with all the new devices to create new kinds of stories and designs.

01

01 / La Chasse, 2014. Photographic series depicting the relationship between species.

02 / HPL, 2010. Photographic series created based on the written works of H.P. Lovecraft. Commissioned by museum La Maison d'Ailleurs in Switzerland and featured in the exhibiton catalogue titled "L'expo qui rend Fou".

02

03 / *Vertebrata, 2011. Photographic series inspired by Marc Da Cunha Lopes' memory of idle display animal skeletons at his university's biology storeroom.*

03

173

Pauline Darley

Photography
Paris

Originally from Burgundy, France, Pauline Darley first engaged in photography at the age of 17. To her, photography is about creating stories around people. Officially launching her photography career in 2010, Darley has teamed up with the makeup whizz at Mademoiselle Mu and produced some of her enduring fashion and beauty shots, such as She has waited too long (2012) and her on-going personal project Halloween collections (2013-). Darley is currently represented by agency Le Crime.

Can you tell us something about your creations?

I like to create with human beings in my photography and articulate their qualities in fashion shots and portraits. I shoot indoor and outdoor, with models, comedians and friends. Sometimes I invent poetic, pop or melancholic universes, and sometimes I choose to stay very clean and natural. Exploring the medium's possibilities non-stop, I refuse to stick to one style all my life. Starting from a few years ago I have been surrounding myself with a loyal team of hairdresser, makeup artist and assistant, who help develop my series a little further in a more extravagant and creative way while enjoying ourselves.

How would you identify your artistic style with French culture?

I admire the work of French painters and illustrators like Gustave Doré and Gustave Moreau, but I am not sure if they have really inspired my work.

How do you usually get yourself ready to create?

I write all my inspirations and ideas I like on a paper notebook. They can be styles, concepts, makeup ideas, atmospheres or light designs. I also ask my team to bring up their ideas and create together!

What makes you stay in France?

I have always lived in France. I stay here because my clients are here, and my agent works in Paris, the city I love. I like walking in the streets of Paris, visiting museums, exhibitions and churches. It sounds very cliché but Paris is a wonderful city. That being said, I would still love to work in other countries!

Where can you find inspiring influences in France?

In movies, magazines, fashion shows, exhibitions, paintings, museums, landscapes, castles...

How would you define French creativity?

I am not in a very objective position to observe what constitutes French creativity, but in my mind it can be inspired by the past; it can be soft, teenage, colourful or in black and white.

What do you plan to do next?

I want to continue with what I do since I started photography. In other words, just make what I want to create. My next project may be something boyish, artistic or soft-toned. But I also dream to have a photo shoot set in a majestic backdrop such as in a castle or a beautiful garden, with real life set design!

02

*01 / She has waited too long, 2012
Fashion design: Valériane Dousse
& Clémentine Levy, makeup: MademoiselleMu, hair: Sophie Haise,
model: Clémentine Levy.*

*02 / Half moon, 2013. Fashion
design: Tatiana Dumabin & Clara,
makeup: MademoiselleMu, hair:
Pierre Saint-Sever using Session
Label OSIS+ Schwarzkopf Professional, model: Gaelle Mancina.
Special credits: Mathyld.*

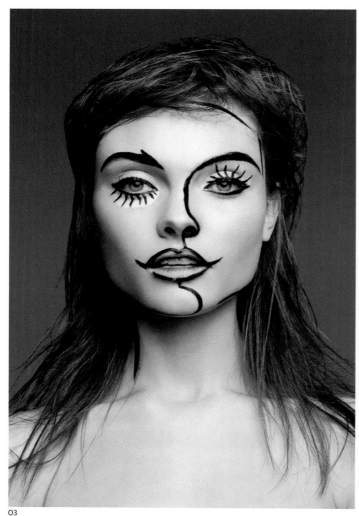

03

03 / Georgie, 2015. Shot with Sony Alpha A7R. makeup: MademoiselleMu, hair: Pierre Saint Sever, model: Georgie @ Metropolitan, retouching: Omen Studio, assistant: Lara Guffroy.

Perrine
Forite

Interactive graphics, illustration
Paris

Having spent a year studying cinema and theatre at La Sorbonne, Perrine Forite jumped creative ship to pursue a career in graphic design. Now a trained graphic designer in the audiovisual and multimedia sphere, with a Master's degree from L'institut Supérieur des Arts Appliqués and solid experience working at agencies in France and abroad, Forite takes up cultural and commercial projects as an independent art director. Her work blends colours and European design influences with creative mediums varying from print to interactive video design.

01

01 / Salon du Pattern, 2015.
Visual identity for a fictional
festival, Pattern.

Can you tell us something about your creations?

I fulfil my clients' wishes through the expression of ideas out of figurative designs.

How would you identify your artistic style with French culture?

Surrounded by French culture, my work is all about diversification.

How do you usually get yourself ready to create?

Before work it is always important for me to surf the internet for a couple of hours to discover new works from around the world. To create we all need inspirations and mine come first from magazines and agencies that I follow online and visit every day. I also have a piece of paper and a pencil nearby to keep myself drawing, it helps a lot to keep myself focused on creative ideas.

What makes you stay in France?

My roots, French culture, talentuous friends, etc. They all feed me energy to work and create. But I'm always looking for new experiences. I do like to travel, live or work in other countries to discover different visual and sound cultures. If any opportunity arises that allow a new experience, I will take it!

Where can you find inspiring influences in France?

Mostly in the street and from temporary exhibitions. But I also exchange a lot of things, for example photography, illustrations and music with people I know.

How would you define French creativity?

For me French creativity is about a shared multicultural innovation. France do have a complex and rich history and we have to take into consideration that this culture is not only about France but also about the surrounding countries that take a major part in forming French culture.

What kind of creative practice would you consider unorthodox in the country?

I think every creative practice has an aim to express ideas and it is very important that they do. I don't have an answer to that because unorthodox or not, each idea has to be told except if it kills!

What do you plan to do next?

One of my next projects is to explore and work on my drawing skills. I dream to develop a career in drawing. I love the idea that you can do everything with just a pen and express figurative ideas. I am experimenting with texture and shapes with just a black pen at the moment, trying to depict all kinds of women's body curves. I will work on different subjects to improve my skills.

02 / Postcards, 2015. Personal
project that aims at marrying
geometrical shades, perspective
and colours.

03 / Batofar, 2015. Visual identity
for Batofar, a concert venue
in Paris.

02

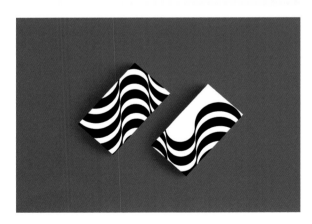

Pierre Jeanneau

Art direction, graphics
Paris / Basque Country

Since 2007, Pierre Jeanneau has built up a design portfolio that stands out on two levels: the substantial amount of campaign posters and flyers he created for arts institutions and Nike, and the close attention he has paid to create original types. With years of experience working at ad agencies and independently as a graphic designer, Jeanneau has developed a signature vocabulary mixing iconography, bright colours and shapes in equal measure. He is now fully devoted to studio work between Paris and the Basque country.

  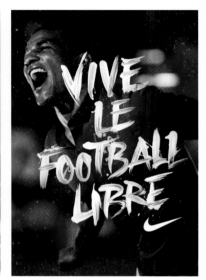

Can you tell us something about your creations?

I always try hard to diversify my approach to graphic design as well as the domains where I apply it, whether it's for advertising, editorial, children's illustration, or cultural venues. Tailored typography is a common strain that holds an important and structural place in my work.

How would you identify your artistic style with French culture?

France has a rich graphic design history and graphic designers of posters have left their mark in pop culture. I have perhaps been influenced by them, but I don't feel particularly linked to French culture. I spend a lot of time in the Basque Country, which has its own strong cultural identity. I also travel as much as possible, my influences are therefore quite varied.

How do you usually get yourself ready to create?

I avoid routine as much as possible since it frightens me. The only rituals I have are coffee and lots of music.

What makes you stay in France?

Family and friends, food, the cultural offerings of Paris, and the numerous landscapes and cultures gathered within a very small land area that make France special.

Where can you find inspiring influences in France ?

Mostly from Paris with its very high density on all levels. I had the chance to meet great art directors in Paris who have insight into iconography and typography which is unusual in the advertising community. They were merging intelligent graphic design with advertising culture.

How would you define French creativity?

Diverse and free.

What kind of creative practice would you consider unorthodox in the country?

None. France is tolerant in that way.

What do you plan to do next?

Keep traveling to find new influences and new projects to apply those influences. I am actually working on part of the interior design for a Parisian sports label Les Halles, an animated book for children and different brand identities. I want to keep diversifying my work.

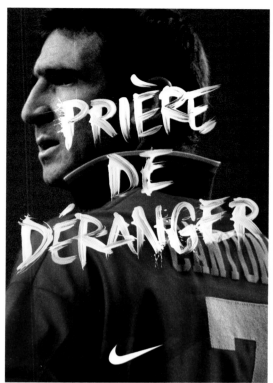

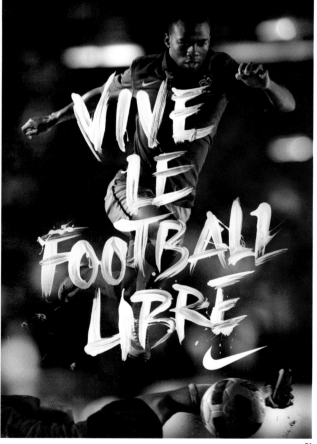

01 / *Vive le Football Libre*, 2011.
Typography for Nike's new
national French soccer team
jersey. AD: Sébastien Pierre,
Pierre Jeanneau. CW: Olivier
Camensuli.

01

NAISSANCE
D'UN CHEF-
D'ŒUVRE
—
BECKETT
GODOT
BLIN

ADAPTATION
ET MISE EN
SCÈNE
STÉPHANIE
CHÉVARA

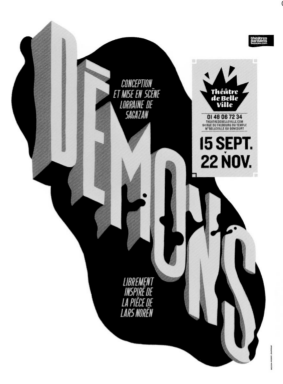

CONCEPTION
ET MISE EN SCÈNE
LORRAINE DE
SAGAZAN

LIBREMENT
INSPIRÉ DE
LA PIÈCE DE
LARS NORÉN

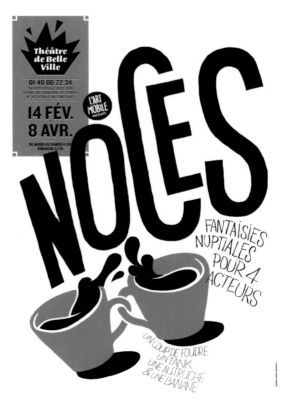

LE THÉÂTRE DIJON BOURGOGNE
CON ET D'UN ACTEUR, L'AUTRE
PRÉSENTENT:

Van Gogh
AUTO-
PORTRAIT

PAR JEAN O'COTTRELL   TEXTES DE VINCENT VAN GOGH
ET ANTONIN ARTAUD

DE MARTIN CRIMP

MISE EN
SCÈNE
RÉMY
BARCHÉ

ÉLOGE DE L'OISIVETÉ

DE DOMINIQUE ROINGVAUX
D'APRÈS BERTRAND RUSSELL
MISE EN SCÈNE
VÉRONIQUE DUMONT

Carmen

Opéra Clownesque

03

PACHA MAMA

Fête du graphisme

CÉLÉBRER PARIS

Pierre Jeanneau
France
2015

Sous le patronage de
Madame Aurélie Filippetti,
ministre de la Culture
et de la Communication

Une Commande artistique
de la Ville de Paris

MAIRIE DE PARIS

Avec JCDecaux, Grand partenaire

JCDecaux

En partenariat avec les professionnels
des arts graphiques

PUBLIS   AGFA

02-03 / *Théâtre de Belleville
programmes & posters, 2011-15.
Art direction and programme
design for Season 12/13, using
blue and gold*

04 / *Pacha mama, 2015. Poster
design for Fête du Graphisme
(Graphics Festival) based on
the theme "Celebrate the Earth",
commissioned by the Mayor
of Paris.*

04

Pierre Sponchiado

Graphics, typography
Paris

Formerly one half of Bornstein & Sponchiado, as a creative director for nine years, Pierre Sponchiado now proposes single solutions that tie ideas greatly to materiality and production techniques. Currently working under the name "Pierre Sponchiado, Design graphique, Paris" created in 2014, the studio specialises in visual communication and is driven by a love for typography. Sponchiado's other expertise includes art direction, signage system, website, photography and type design.

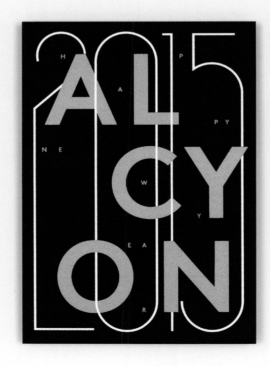

01 / Alcyon Groupe Greeting Card,
2015. A poster-card blends new year
wishes with the year 2015 and the
data network provider's name.

Can you tell us something about your creations?

Each project is unique, and every time I try to go as far as I can in terms of graphic experimentation. I seek above all to find a real visual pleasure and harmony of tones that give strength to the project.

How would you identify your artistic style with French culture?

I belong to the younger generation of designers who are fed by the same codes and references, and based on which we develop our own universe. As for me, I build my work around typography which I like to draw and play with scale and spacing. I also give my work a sense of elegance and fine details, which seem to cohere with our culture.

How do you usually get yourself ready to create?

I focus primarily on the emotion which the final draft conveys — how the colours and visual strength set the mood in line with my client's needs? I always start with typography, visualising the main colours and roughly the forms. I always begin with my pencil and paper. It helps me map out my ideas quickly, without going into details.

What makes you stay in France?

Family, friends and food.

Where can you find inspiring influences in France?

Everywhere, but especially in the street I think. I look at absolutely everything and retain what interests me most — posters, the city's signs, the ambiance of a place, the colours of Paris, etc. Then, obviously, I follow some blogs dedicated to graphic design, fashion, design, art and architecture, since all these disciplines are interrelated.

How would you define French creativity?

French creativity is founded on its culture. A plural culture. Its richness derives from its history, its people and cannot simply be defined. There are so many streams as are designers. Is it not a certain idea of the art of French living which ultimately spurs prolific exploration, for better or worse? This French creativity inevitably confronts the public, who are still not ready for changes on the whole when compared with other countries where design is part of everyday life. Pity?

What kind of creative practice would you consider unorthodox in the country?

I always have the impression that we are a bit behind the Anglo-Saxons countries. Not physically but the tools we use for production and the way we organise work.

What do you plan to do next?

I will of course continue to explore typography, irrespective of the medium. Whether it's intended to be signage or a logotype on the back of a business card, the fun is the same. I am very inquisitive by nature, so I would like to make some videos and animations too, soon.

02 / Paris Batignolles Aménagement Greeting Cards, 2015. Packages carry the latest figures, data and photo about an urban development project, Clichy-Batignolles, managed by PBA.

03 / Celebrating Earth – Welcome Home, 2015. Poster gives a nod to the Paris Climate Change conference (COP21) 2015 as part of a design campaign.

02

*04 / Smart-it Visual Identity,
2015. Graphic identity articulates
the IT specialist's knowledge in
networks, cloud services and
data systems.*

05 / *Loïc Picquet Atelier Architects Visual Identity,
2015. A daring play of lettering creates a rhythm
suggestive of space and fitting linked to the work of
the architects.*

LOÏC PICQUET
ATELIER
ARCHITECTES

Say What
Studio

Art direction, graphics
Paris

Established in 2011, Say What Studio is a creative partnership between Benoit Berger and Nathalie Kapagiannidi, both graduates of École de Communication Visuelle, Paris. Tied by a love for print matters, the art directors use their craftsmanship instinct to redefine brand and visual experiences through their fashionable choice of types, imagery and editorial designs. Apart from their design studio, the duo also runs design blog, Mirador.

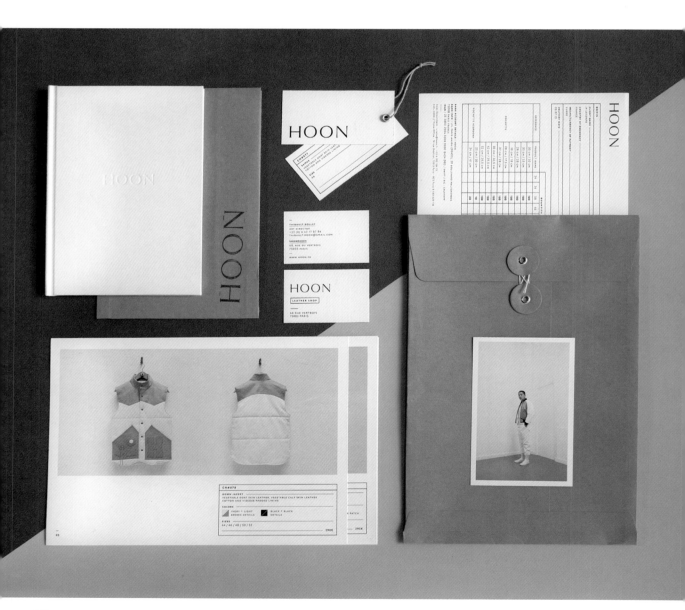

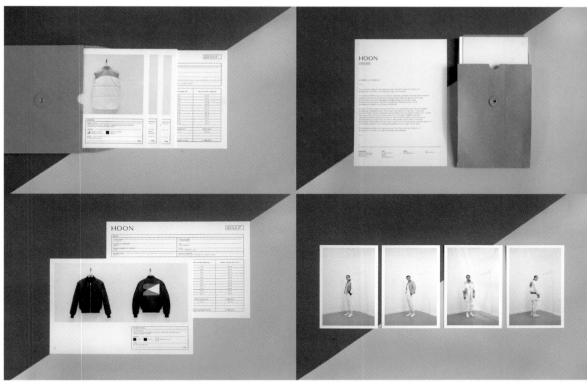

01 / Hoon Leather Shop, 2015.
Logotype, branding, editorial
and website design for a Parisian
brand.

Can you tell us something about your creations?

We consider graphic design as a discipline that needs to be maintained. Learning and gaining experience is an ongoing process, and our skills can always be sharpened. We therefore strive to try out new techniques and question our achievements thoroughly so that our creative process evolves continually. We seek to produce uncluttered and minimalist design that is strong and recognisable at once. Each of our project helps to develop and refine our creative universe, which we later try to inject into our new designs. The coherence between our projects is essential.

How would you identify your artistic style with French culture?

French fine arts have been around for centuries, but if we give it some time, the public's eye will become accustomed to the French new era and to what this new generation has to offer. The local design scene is very active, with many names, studios and collectives working and operating in their own distinctive styles. There is no real competition but rather collective advances that allow Parisian design to wear many styles and speak more and more of its creators. The design we provide is the right mix between traditional and contemporary styles, so we can identity with the new era of French culture.

What makes you stay in France?

We were both raised in the French culture and met in Paris in 2007 at the beginning of our studies. We wanted to create something of our own upon graduation and that's how our studio was born. We have been based in Paris ever since, but the kind of work we do doesn't bind us a to a specific place. Travelling is always on the table. We'd be thrilled to discover new places, or meet with our international clients mainly based in the US with whom we have been working for a while.

How would you define French creativity?

French designers have always brought special care to their products, design and the final aspect of each project. We believe that French design thrives internationally because it's part of a comprehensive approach of unique design, production, craftsmanship and finesse. In particular, we believe many French luxury brands are pushing their image and partnering artists ever further, and that is an exemplar of French creativity.

What kind of creative practice would you consider unorthodox in the country?

Probably glitch art. Defined by digital and analogue errors or "bugs", this "visual corruption" is still a marginal practice.

What do you plan to do next?

We're currently working on many new projects, especially a new brand we'd like to launch in 2016. It's something that has been on our mind since we put our self-initiated brand Avalanche on pause, and we think now is the time to start a new adventure.

02 / Démocratie, 2015. Branding for Parisian concept-store Démocratie.

03 / Dénature, 2014. Stencil on patterned cloth.

02

04

04 / Apartment A, 2013. Art direction and branding for event space Apartment A and gallery bar Cocktail Academy in Los Angeles, US.

Solène Lebon-Couturier

Illustration, textile art
Paris

Born in 1981 in Léhon, Brittany, Solène Lebon-Couturier brings her playful imagination and powers of observation to areas of fashion, editorial and theatre. Friends as well as contemporary artists like Malika Favre and burlesque dancer Charly Broutille have contributed significant influences to her art, through which she celebrates femininity and bonds of friendship. In 2008, Lebon-Couturier co-founded Collectif France Tricot with Emmanuelle Barrère. Together they start yarn bombing in various parts of France and Germany.

01

01 / Hot, 2015. Knitted illustration for Milk x Magazine issue "Hot".

02 / Red shoes, 2015. Knitted illustration as a wink to Chanel style.

03 / Pin up, 2014. Knitted illustration reinterprets a Malika Favre illustration.

Can you tell us something about your creations?

My creations are all hand-knitted. I mix several knitting techniques to create photographic images, one of which is intarsia. Sometimes I knit sculptural pieces for installations. Most of the portraits I created are tributes to people whose work I admire. I also like telling stories with my knitting. This includes L'effeuillée, a series about striptease, and Triptyque, which is my most personal piece on birth and death.

How would you identify your artistic style with French culture?

I think knitting is something universal, but maybe the textile medium, combined with bold colours and the photographic way I knit can create a relationship with fashion and match with the long historical fashion heritage we have in France. I learnt that during the French Revolution, some women knitted while attending the guillotine executions. Nice, isn't it?

How do you usually get yourself ready to create?

I get my yarn, a big cup of coffee or tea (Choco Chili, yum!), my needles and my computer ready. Sometimes I watch a documentary or a silly programme on TV at the same time. And that's it!

What makes you stay in France?

I love living in Paris even if I miss Brittany sometimes. Paris is full of inspiring people and exhibitions — such an inspiring city that I can live with its negative aspects. My roots are in France. I love travelling too but when I stay abroad for too long I feel homesick. Probably because I miss the cheese, wine, good bread and salted butter. I can't live without them!

Where can you find inspiring influences in France?

Everywhere, but I have to admit that talented people inspire me a lot, such as Emmanuelle Esther, Malika Favre, Alexandra Bruel and Charly Broutille, to name a few. I like to make portraits of people who create work that I admire. I use the internet to explore a lot of other people's work in very different fields. I like to generate tangible representations derived from a digital relationship.

How would you define French creativity?

Fresh, joyful, unconventional, fun with no fear for embrassing the old-fashioned.

What kind of creative practice would you consider unorthodox in the country?

It's very difficult to say what's the most unorthodox because there are too many, but that's not a bad thing! Hijacking the orthodox is a good start. Using materials in a new way — playing with classical practices and distorting traditions — is what makes art progress, in my opinion.

What do you plan to do next?

I want to keep working with yarn, and tell more stories with knitted pictures. I've started one with a pole dancer, and I want to finish it.

01 / Hot, 2015. Knitted illustration for Milk x Magazine issue "Hot".   *02 / Red shoes, 2015. Knitted illustration as a wink to Chanel style.*   *03 / Pin up, 2014. Knitted illustration reinterprets a Malika Favre illustration.*

Can you tell us something about your creations?

My creations are all hand-knitted. I mix several knitting techniques to create photographic images, one of which is intarsia. Sometimes I knit sculptural pieces for installations. Most of the portraits I created are tributes to people whose work I admire. I also like telling stories with my knitting. This includes L'effeuillée, a series about striptease, and Triptyque, which is my most personal piece on birth and death.

How would you identify your artistic style with French culture?

I think knitting is something universal, but maybe the textile medium, combined with bold colours and the photographic way I knit can create a relationship with fashion and match with the long historical fashion heritage we have in France. I learnt that during the French Revolution, some women knitted while attending the guillotine executions. Nice, isn't it?

How do you usually get yourself ready to create?

I get my yarn, a big cup of coffee or tea (Choco Chili, yum!), my needles and my computer ready. Sometimes I watch a documentary or a silly programme on TV at the same time. And that's it!

What makes you stay in France?

I love living in Paris even if I miss Brittany sometimes. Paris is full of inspiring people and exhibitions — such an inspiring city that I can live with its negative aspects. My roots are in France. I love travelling too but when I stay abroad for too long I feel homesick. Probably because I miss the cheese, wine, good bread and salted butter. I can't live without them!

Where can you find inspiring influences in France?

Everywhere, but I have to admit that talented people inspire me a lot, such as Emmanuelle Esther, Malika Favre, Alexandra Bruel and Charly Broutille, to name a few. I like to make portraits of people who create work that I admire. I use the internet to explore a lot of other people's work in very different fields. I like to generate tangible representations derived from a digital relationship.

How would you define French creativity?

Fresh, joyful, unconventional, fun with no fear for embrassing the old-fashioned.

What kind of creative practice would you consider unorthodox in the country?

It's very difficult to say what's the most unorthodox because there are too many, but that's not a bad thing! Hijacking the orthodox is a good start. Using materials in a new way — playing with classical practices and distorting traditions — is what makes art progress, in my opinion.

What do you plan to do next?

I want to keep working with yarn, and tell more stories with knitted pictures. I've started one with a pole dancer, and I want to finish it.

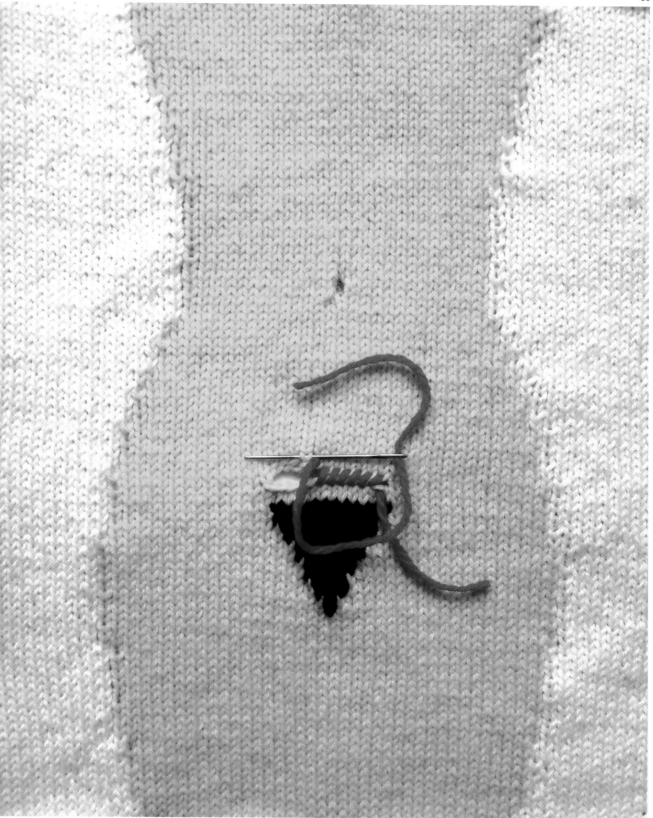

04 / Natacha, 2015. Private commission. Portrait of Natacha in Los Angeles.

05 / Charly Broutille, 2014. Portrait of French burlesque artist, Charly Broutille.

06 / Triptyque: La couture, 2014. One of the three illustrations about motherhood for Collectif Vingtaine.

07 / Lisa, 2014. Portrait of Lisa Gachet, author of French blog, Make my lemonade.

08 / Senyor Pablo, 2014. Portrait of Spanish designer and knitter, Senyor Pablo, from Madrid.

09 / Alexandra, 2014. Portrait of French artist Alexandra Bruel.

10 / Carrie, 2014. Knitted version of a Malika Favre illustration inspired by Brian de Palma's movie.

10

07

08

09

Studio Dessuant Bone

Graphics, furniture design, scenography
Paris

Coming from different design disciplines but sharing a common bond to design, Marie Dessuant and Philip Bone co-founded Studio Dessuant Bone in Paris in 2014. The duo has known each other at Fabrica, back in 2011. With their specialities in art direction, interiors and product design, they pride themselves on producing solutions that traverse the fields of fashion and lifestyle from concept to design. Recent projects include photography and set design for Celine, and conceptual collection "Fasted" featured at Salone Del Mobile 2015.

01

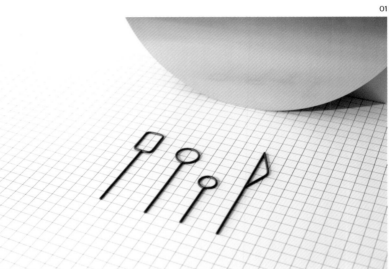

Can you tell us something about your creations?

Studio Dessuant Bone is a multidisciplinary design consultancy based in Paris. We specialise in direction, design, product and interiors, providing research-based creative solutions that evolve from ideas and stories. We pride ourselves in creating engaging and clear handwritings that traverse a diverse range of clients and industries, including fashion, lifestyle and product, from concept to creation.

How would you identify your artistic style with French culture?

One of our strengths is that we come from two different cultures. However we both have lived abroad in Italy and China as well. We try not to limit ourself to British or French cultures.

How do you usually get yourself ready to create?

We always start by talking through concepts, ideas and meanings of a project before drawing or sketching anything. After this process comes visual direction.

What makes you come to France?

We came to Paris in 2014 to start our studio. It is a place with amazing cultural offerings, great lifestyle and an emergence of a new dynamic creative scene. We also work often in London because we love the incredible energy there.

Where can you find inspiring influences in France?

We love Gallery S. Bensimon and NextLevel Gallery for their effort to integrate art and design. We also enjoy visiting museums and galleries such as Palais de Tokyo, Galerie du Jeu de Paume or Musée d'Art Moderne de la Ville de Paris.

How would you define French creativity?

It does not only lay emphasis on efficiency and functionality, but also elegance and refinement.

What kind of creative practice would you consider unorthodox in the country?

Small practices that work with different disciplines and are open to embracing different media.

What do you plan to do next?

We are working on our new show at VV Gallery in Brussels at the moment. We will continue to explore a creative approach that breaks the barriers between design, art and fashion worlds.

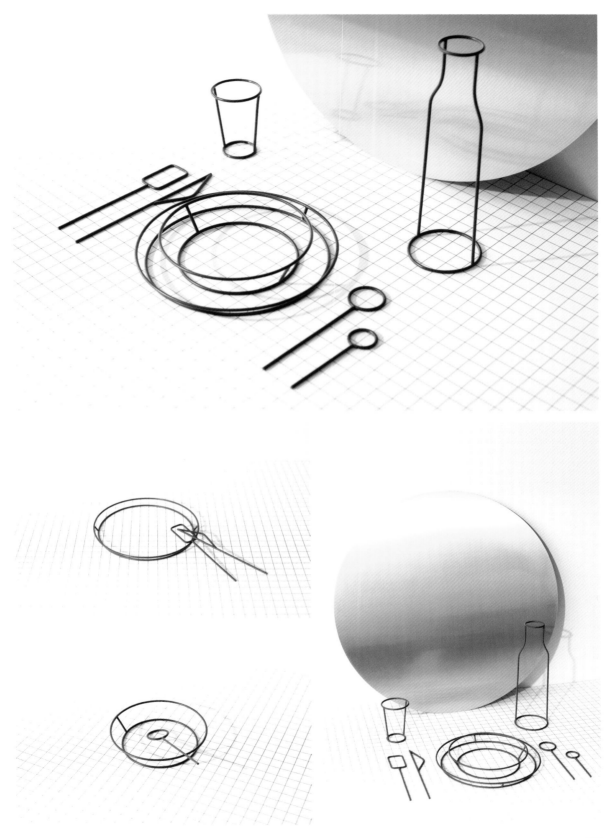

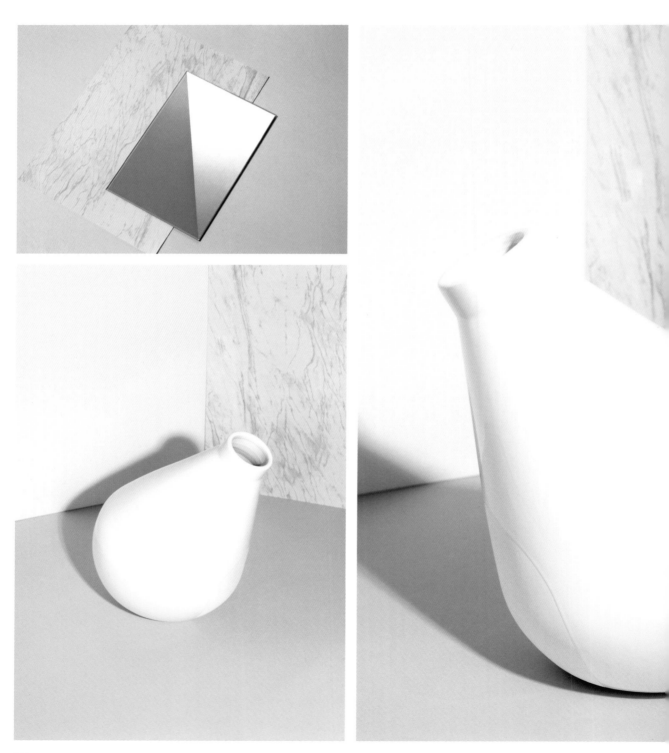

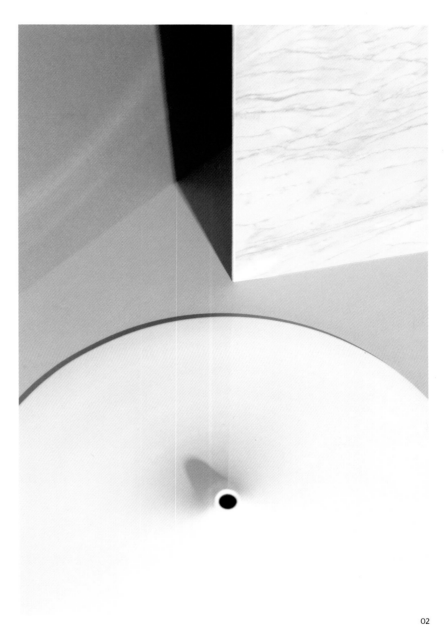

01 / Fasted, 2015. Product and conceptual design produced as part of the exhibition 'A Stomaco Vuoto' curated by DWA Studio.

02 / The Bay Collection, 2013. Two vases and a collection of silk-screened mirrors developed with a limited edition for Singulartie.

03 / Objet Prefere, 2012. Installation and product design developed as a response to "What is your favourite object?" for Grand-Hornu Museum, Belgium, as part of Fabrica's team.

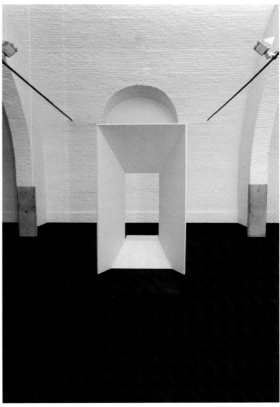

Studio
My Name
is Wendy

Art direction, graphics
Paris

Born in 2006, Studio My Name is Wendy comprises of graphic designers Carole Gautier and Eugénie Favre. Through collaborations, the pair brings together their expertise in graphic design and visual arts to produce some of the most eye-catching visual identities, exhibition posters, patterns and editorial designs that meld modern aesthetics with surrealist collage. On the side, MNISW also publishes limited prints and recently a strategy-based board game named Byland.

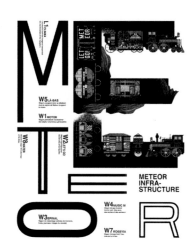

Can you tell us something about your creations?

We love to build things. A 'structure' underpins everything we do. Through this structure, we work on successive layers of senses that are more or less deep, some crumpled up and others touch. We do not create points but rather knots of access that encourage open thinking, questioning and diverse perspectives. Of course, describing our design as narrative would correspond to our approach, but there is also a dimension of presence in forms, tones, objects, texts and titles. For us, it is important that viewers of our creations feel invited.

What makes you stay in France?

From time to time we think about leaving France to see what's happening elsewhere, and to see what it's like when graphic design is more respected with a clearer and more established economic dimension abroad. But we also have this urge to witness the changes being made in France and to participate in them when they occur.

Where can you find inspiring influences in France?

Contemporary art, poetry and the cinema influence us, really. Also through monographic publications of major graphic designers. Poetry can be the strangest influence but there is something very interesting about the displacement of constraints, codes, language, and concern to instill sense and rhythm. We love making graphic design more flexible, elastic, hard or porous without weakening readability. No,

absolutely not, as there is another way of reading by another speed that works cleverly to deliver meanings and connect with people.

How would you define French creativity?

This is not an easy question. We believe that there is a legacy created by avant garde artists but it became political in the 1960s. There is an undeniable trend about French graphic design flirting with art. French graphic design is less direct in message delivery, and possesses a certain ambiguity which is associated with our visual culture.

What kind of creative practice would you consider unorthodox in the country?

Unfortunately, we think that France is rather orthodox in many areas at present. The innovative and well thought out creations we encounter here are sometimes produced somewhere else. We follow the example in a broad sense, from cinema and music to ecology and science. It is undeniable that there are creators in France, but the French system is very closed and therefore it is difficult for a project to stand out.

What do you plan to do next?

We are working on My Name is Jack, the studio's shop that sells limited edition posters and unique design objects and hosts exhibitions where artists can raise questions on both of our practices.

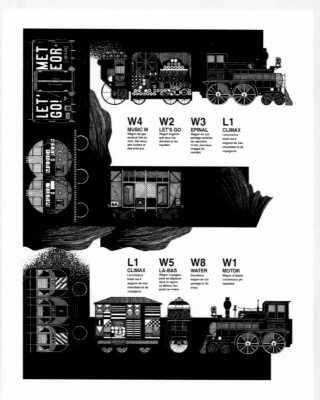

02

01 / Meteor Project / Infrastructure, 2013-. Experimental studio project.

02 / Mallarme's Books, 2015. Poster collection about book and reading space as a tribute to Stéphane Mallarmé.

ESPACE DE L'ECTURE

NOTES EN VUE DU LIVRE

CE BLOC NE PEUT DONC AUCUNEMENT FAIRE UN CARRÉ
QUE DE FAÇADE, EN VOYANT LES DOS, PAR EXEMPLE, SOIT DEBOUT
SOIT COUCHE—MAIS IL NE L'AURA PAS EN PROFONDEUR OU—EN CE QUI.
QUAND ON LE CONSIDERE D'EN FACE, DEVIENDRA EPAISSEUR
(RAPPORT DE L'EPAISSEUR DU LIVRE ET DE SA LARGEUR PAR DEUX FOIS
COUCHE OU DEBOUT D'OU LA SIGNALER D'OR—ELLE RESTE LA MEME TRAIT D'OU.
EN TRACER EN EPAISSEUR ET LARGEUR DONNEE AUSSI
EXACTEMENT AUSSI SERRÉE QUE POSSIBLE.

IL FAUDRA QUE CES SURFACES VOL. SOIENT LES MÊMES—MAIS
DIFFÉREMMENT DISPOSÉES—(L   L OU L   L ?)
POUR ÉTABLIR UNE IDENTITE
L'IG. ETANT QUE ETANT DONNÉE DEUX FOIS.
LES RAPPORTS N'AYANT D'AUTRE BUT QUE DE MONTRER
FIXER UN PRIX ETC. MAIS PAR CELA MÊME N'INDIQUANT À
L'AUTEUR

S. MALLARMÉ

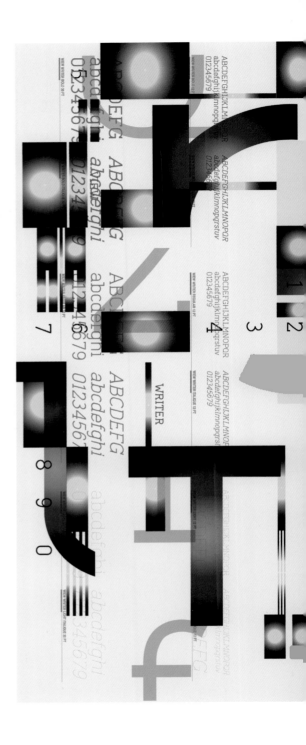

03

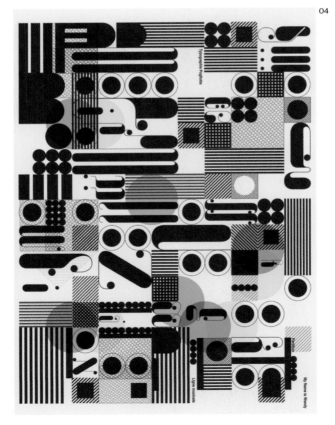

04

03 / Meteor Project Poster, 2013-. Ongoing experimental studio project.

04 / Pogliotte Poster, 2014. Studio project exploring with 'Pogliotte', a typeface constructed in-house on the basis of musical line and notation.

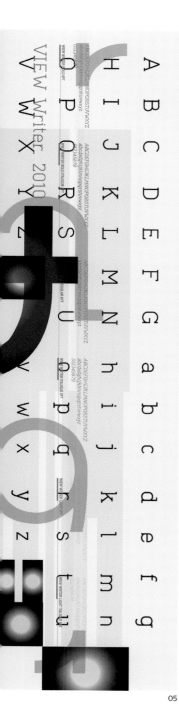

05

06

05 / View-Writer Poster, 2014.
Studio project exploring with in-
house typeface 'View-Writer'.

06 / Ficciones Typografika, 2015.
A project dedicated to typographic exploration in a public
space curated by Erik Brandt.

Studio Paris se quema

Art direction, scenography, animation
Paris

Anaïs Harel and Nicolas Ocante form Studio Paris se quema. Formerly co-workers at eco-fashion brand Veja and Parisian concept store Centre Commercial as in-house art directors, the pair united their creative force in 2014 to produce contemporary solutions crowned by their appetite for colour, anamorphosis, trompe-l'oeil, geometry, materials and references to all kinds of classic and contemporary arts. Paris se quema is represented by Barelly Studio.

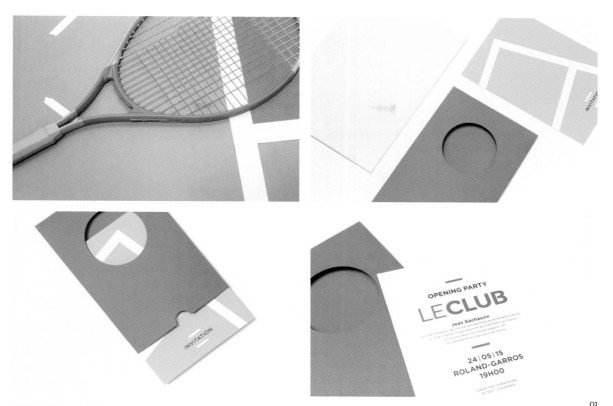

01

01 / Roland Garros - Le Club, 2015. Printed and gif invitation for Le Club opening at Roland Garros Stadium.

Can you tell us something about your creations?

Our aim is to work in very different realms of design that go from print, photography and graphic design, to web design and scenography. We try to respond to our customers' needs and constraints while keeping our obsession with colour, geometry and trompe l'oeil satisfied. We take this as a guideline, not a dogma. We are not going after specialisation, though sometimes it comes by itself.

How would you identify your artistic style with French culture?

It's hard to answer this question as two French people, but we love everything related to manual work, crafts and materials 'savoir-faire': paper, wood, leather… We give importance to time. We enjoy the process that leads to the final results.

How do you usually get yourself ready to create?

Sometimes we look at a lot of images before actually getting down to work. It's best when the ideas come by themselves during a conversation, preferably outside the office, on a shoot or at lunch. Then we make quick sketches in a notebook and things follow. It's always fun to come back to the sketches afterwards, realising how everything just started there. But sometimes when time is tight, we need to force ourselves to find the idea right away.

What makes you stay in France?

Paris is in the name of our studio so that says a lot. We love this city and we do not feel cramped here for now. Things are happening here.

Many of our friends have created companies, brands and magazines around us. We have the feeling that creativity is all around us in Paris and it feeds our ambitions too.

Where can you find inspiring influences in France?

There is a genuine artistic scene here. Arts, cinema, music, fashion — the combination of all these talents inspire us every day.

How would you define French creativity?

We do not believe creativity has a nationality today. The creative people we follow on social networks or whose work we admire in books or magazines are from different countries. There are different trends and styles, but we do not find that they are significantly influenced by their country. What varies between countries is more about the recognition given to the savoir-faire: how well people know that what we do is not merely related to the use of software.

What kind of creative practice would you consider unorthodox in the country?

What appears unorthodox to us here is the gap between graphic design and advertising.

What do you plan to do next?

We are used to working with still images, so we are eager to work more with motion graphics and videos.

02 / *Kaleidoscope*, 2015. Art
direction and set design for food
and travel magazine, Mint.

03 / *Superbox*, 2015. Art direction, photography and set design
for Milk Magazine.

03

04 / Kalpakian x Galerie BSL,
2014. Art direction, set design
and photography of Moon
armchair designed by Charles
Kalpakian, edited by BSL Gallery.

04

05 / Art Mobile(s), 2015.
Self-published project design
resumes the codes of the great
20th century artistic movements
for children.

Thibaud Sabathier

Graphics, interactive graphics
Paris / Amsterdam

Graduating with a Master's degree in digital design from Ecole de Communication Visuelle (ECV) in Bordeaux in 2015, Thibaud Sabathier has already built a diverse portfolio featuring well-executed school work and spec jobs that deal with visual communications and interactive experiences. Parallel to his freelance work, the young French graphic designer has worked at Hi-ReS New York (US) as interactive designer trainee and graphic design intern at Thonik (Amsterdam, the Netherlands).

Can you tell us something about your creations?

I consider myself a designer rather than a graphic designer. I try to bring my point of view into my projects, and develop a graphic language that can generate powerful solutions and a coherent message to meet specific requests. My creative process can be pictured as a clear, systematic architectural structure with the maxim 'Less but better'. A structure that creates efficient design with less information as a tribute to the inspiring work of Dieter Rams. Also, the use of material plays an important role in my design process.

How would you identify your artistic style with French culture?

More than a style my work projects my design philosophy. Thanks to the digital age, my philosophy is shaped by international influences as well as ideas from the modernism period. That being said, the global identity appears in my work is constructed by an eclectic vision of the world nurtured by the French culture.

How do you usually get yourself ready to create?

I read a lot of magazines and books. Old modernist brochures I collect or old books that I found over the weekend can feed me inspirations before I start any projects. Whether sketching on a grid for a poster or wireframing a website, working on paper will helpfully stimulate fresh ideas before I start the computer. But the most important thing to get myself ready to work each day is to be passionate about what I do.

What makes you stay in France?

I'm going to set up my office in France as this is where artists like Van Gogh and Picasso were attracted to stay and work on their craft.

Where can you find inspiring influences in France?

French culture is inspiring because of its diversity. I find inspirations in fine art, contemporary art and the fashion world. The encouragingly vibrant illustration scene here will force creatives to push the boundaries of expression. I am inspired by the work of Henri Matisse and Pablo Picasso as well as Malika Favre and Nous Vous but influences are everywhere beyond the French territory. I am stimulated by my travels, vinyl covers and also food on my plate.

How would you define French creativity?

The French artistic fields are diverse, fertile and well-known. Its cinema, fashion, music and design offer an eminent personality that inspires and motivates the next generation of designers like me.

What do you plan to do next?

I am between my personal and company work, learning skills from experienced creatives. I want to participate in more design exhibitions, conferences and start teaching in a few years' time to share my skills. I also keep in mind the idea to return to our roots and set up a studio in Bordeaux with my friend Florent Gomez.

01 / Henri Matisse Tribute, 2014. Personal work as a tribute to the special work of Henri Matisse based on cuts-out.

02 / Landscape of Programming Languages, 2014. Visualisations and infographics inspired by particles accelerator of CERN and constellations paths.

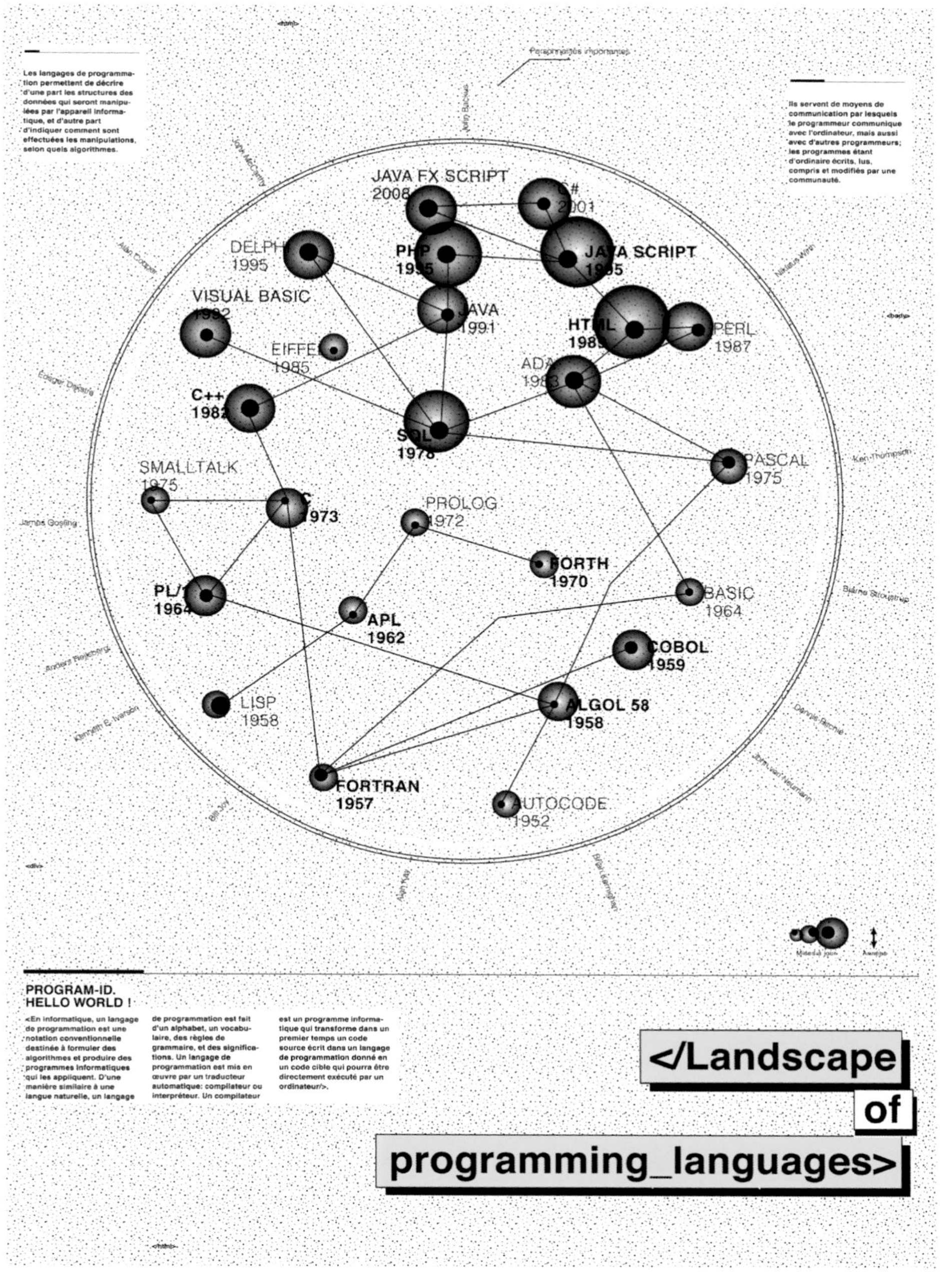
Les langages de programmation permettent de décrire d'une part les structures des données qui seront manipulées par l'appareil informatique, et d'autre part d'indiquer comment sont effectuées les manipulations, selon quels algorithmes.
Ils servent de moyens de communication par lesquels le programmeur communique avec l'ordinateur, mais aussi avec d'autres programmeurs; les programmes étant d'ordinaire écrits, lus, compris et modifiés par une communauté.
JAVA FX SCRIPT 2008
C# 2001
PHP 1995
JAVA SCRIPT 1995
DELPHI 1995
VISUAL BASIC 1992
JAVA 1991
HTML 1989
PERL 1987
EIFFEL 1985
ADA 1983
C++ 1982
SQL 1978
SMALLTALK 1975
PASCAL 1975
C 1973
PROLOG 1972
FORTH 1970
PL/1 1964
BASIC 1964
APL 1962
COBOL 1959
LISP 1958
ALGOL 58 1958
FORTRAN 1957
AUTOCODE 1952
Niklaus Wirth
Ken Thompson
James Gosling
PROGRAM-ID. HELLO WORLD !
«En informatique, un langage de programmation est une notation conventionnelle destinée à formuler des algorithmes et produire des programmes informatiques qui les appliquent. D'une manière similaire à une langue naturelle, un langage de programmation est fait d'un alphabet, un vocabulaire, des règles de grammaire, et des significations. Un langage de programmation est mis en œuvre par un traducteur automatique: compilateur ou interpréteur. Un compilateur est un programme informatique qui transforme dans un premier temps un code source écrit dans un langage de programmation donné en un code cible qui pourra être directement exécuté par un ordinateur/>.
</Landscape of programming_languages>

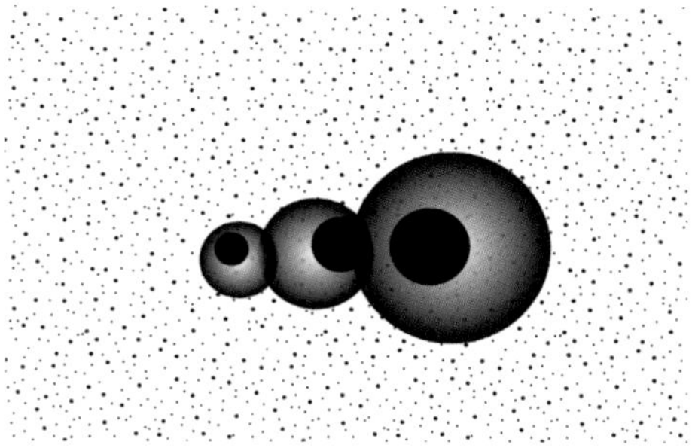

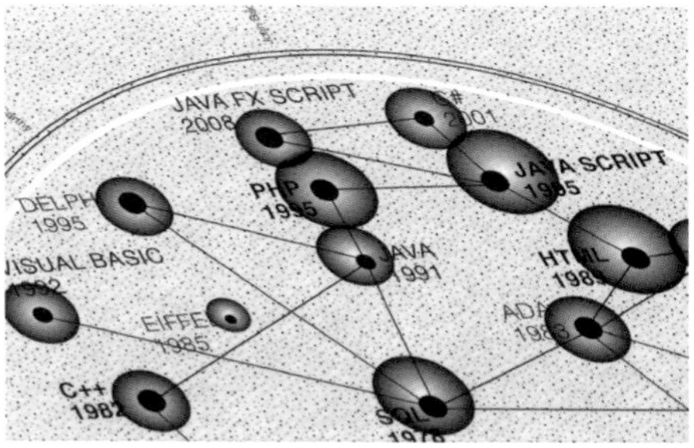
JAVA FX SCRIPT 2008
PHP 1995
JAVA SCRIPT 1995
DELPHI 1995
VISUAL BASIC
JAVA 1991
EIFFEL 1985
C++ 1982

02

03 / Le Méliès, 2014. Branding, poster and web design for multi-cultural place Le Méliès.

04 / Interactive Poster, 2015. A short programme developed with processing for an exhibition at ECV school.

05 / The Other New York Project, 2014. Personal experimentations of a journey in New York City.

03

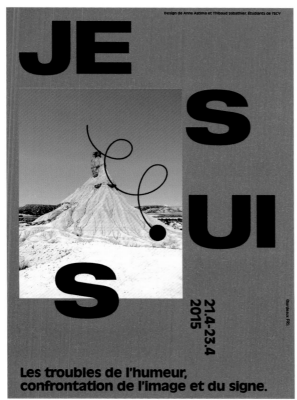

JE S UI S

21.4-23.4
2015

(bordeaux FR).

Les troubles de l'humeur, confrontation de l'image et du signe.

J'AIM E

21.4-23.4
2015

(bordeaux FR).

Les troubles de l'humeur, confrontation de l'image et du signe.

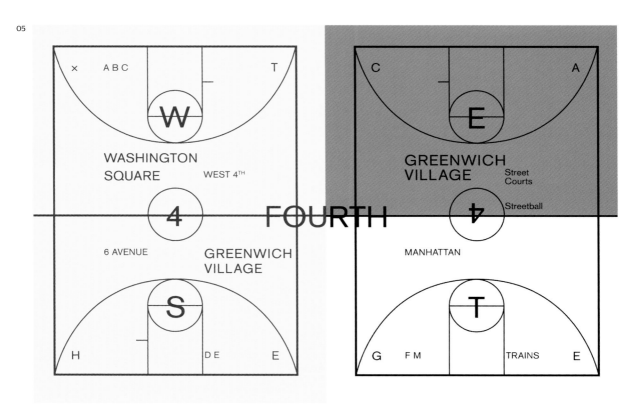

× A B C   T

W

WASHINGTON
SQUARE   WEST 4TH

4   FOURTH

6 AVENUE   GREENWICH
VILLAGE

S

H   D E   E

C   A

E

GREENWICH
VILLAGE   Street
Courts

4   Streetball

MANHATTAN

T

G   F M   TRAINS   E

Thibault Delhom

Photography, digital art
Paris

Thibault Delhom's first step to become an image-maker was one year of professional training in graphic communications before switching to pursue photography in 2010. In only five years' time, the photographer has built an impressive body of work, suggesting that his skills, from the ways he handled light and shadows, contrasts and photo-editing to overplay human characters, have gone from strength to strength. Since Delhom entered his photography realm, he has established work relationships with the likes of Beaux Arts De Paris and Kitsuné Journal.

01 / *Asphixie, 2015*

Can you tell us something about your creations?

My main source of inspiration is human. I like to analyse feelings and behaviours as they emerge. I work a lot around anxiety, oppression and dehumanisation. I cannot define my work other than through crafting, testing and learning. This is a field of work that should not linger over the already acquired. And I would not defend otherwise, even if they are denigrated. My images may seem touching to some people, but they can also give a sloppy and immature impression to others. My work can be defined by such divergent opinions and is only translated by the ones who pay attention. My own definition is definitely more neutral. What I can be sure of is that my work defines me and helps me move forward on a daily basis. This is my therapy, my way of seeing the world and how I entertain myself.

How would you identify your artistic style with French culture?

I do not see any connection between my artistic style and the French culture. My work explores dehumanisation, depression, anxiety, loneliness, modern slavery, social depression and the loss of identity. My images reflect the vision I have of the world, and not that of France. My influences are global. To me, every curve impresses and exudes a certain emotion. As a sign language, everything revolves and makes sense according to the impact of lines and placements. I retouch images mainly to reshape — either mitigate or accentuate curves while exaggerating the reality. My work is partly based on the aesthetic way of seeing things.

How do you usually get yourself ready to create?

I do not think I have a particular creative routine. I take things as they come, according to my desires at the moment.

What makes you stay in France?

I work in France at the moment because I like to be with my close friends and family. But I would like to travel abroad for projects.

Where can you find inspiring influences in France?

My influences are not necessarily French. I think I am influenced by independent artists around the world that are not formatted by their education or job, such as Jean-François Lepage from France and Natalia Evelyn Bencicova from Slovakia.

How would you define French creativity?

I cannot define the French creativity. Creativity, like everything else, has no boundaries…

What do you plan to do next?

I wish to continue with my projects in photography, and also in film and music. I am currently working on sound projects to complement the videos that I have done.

02 / *False Freedom, 2013*

03 / Naked Discovery, 2013

04 / *Touch Of Hope, 2014*

05 / *Phasis, 2014*

Twice

Art direction, graphics
Paris

From poster campaigns to graphic identities and publishing projects, Twice manifests a special tie with music, fashion and other arts and cultural events. Their shape eyes for details and strong attachment to the creative fields are perceivable in their material choice, pattern design and production handled with meticulous care. Twice co-founders Fanny Le Bras and Clémentine Berry have worked jointly and independently before their partnership came to life. Together they have a prominent client base made of the likes of Hermès, la Gaîté Lyrique and Universal Music.

01 / Design Parade 9, 2014. Visual
identity and catalogue for house
museum la villa Noailles, Hyères.

Can you tell us something about your creations?

Our creations are the fruit of our two spirits and sensibilities, our collaborations and discussions.

How would you identify your artistic style with French culture?

We do not have a fixed identifiable style, but we aim to frame our projects within historic references (works by Le Corbusier, Eileen Grey or Sonia Delaunay, to name a few) and within the needs of our clients. We do not think there is a particular French style. Today we are more or less influenced by all the cultures around us. Japan, Korea, the Anglo-Saxon countries, and the States are all inspirations for us.

How do you usually get yourself ready to create?

We usually start with a brainstorming session between the two of us, and then proceed to sessions of drawing. Our work is tangible and manual. We use the painting tools, Chinese inks, scanned images, fabrics, or any other materials that fall into our hands. After this process, we digitalise what we need and rework our ideas on the computer.

What makes you stay in France?

We grew up in France, studied in Paris and thus naturally created our studio here.

Where can you find inspiring influences in France?

For hundreds of years, the history of our country has been filled with iconic images and forms. We love the paintings of Sonia Delaunay, the works of Modernist architects, as well as silly videos on Youtube and contemporary art. Everything around us can be a source of inspiration.

How would you define French creativity?

We do not think there is a particular type of 'French creativity' but more of a creative aura which bonds creative minds of our generation that are exposed to the same influences, have the same instincts and desires to communicate with the world.

What kind of creative practice would you consider unorthodox in the country?

Creativity in general is unorthodox. We feel like the more surprising practices often come from small studios, regardless of their domain or their geographic location. We think that nowadays, creative practices are emerging from around the world and it feels weird to single out creativity from a particular country.

What do you plan to do next?

We would love to explore space and work more in detail on scenographic projects. We are also working on the second edition of our self-published magazine, Contraintes. You can still get the last copies of the first edition on www.revuecontraintes.fr. The design of the second edition will be different but we will keep it as a surprise for now!

Aurélie Filippetti, ministre de la Culture
et de la Communication
Hubert Falco, ancien ministre,
président de la communauté d'agglomérat
Toulon Provence Méditerranée
Jacques Politi, maire de la Ville d'Hyères,
conseiller général du Var,
Michel Vauzelle, président du Conseil
Régional Provence-Alpes-Côte d'Azur
Horace Lanfranchi, président
du Conseil Général du Var
Jean-Sébastien Vialatte, président de

d'agglomération Toulon Provence Méditerranée
Didier Grumbach, président
de l'Association villa Noailles
Pascale Mussard, présidente de
l'Association des Amis de Saint Bernard
Jean Pierre Blanc, directeur
du centre d'art villa Noailles
Le bureau et les conseillers communautaires
de Toulon Provence Méditerranée

Architectures pour l'avenir

02

02 / *Architecture pour l'avenir,
2014 Visual Identity and
catalogue for exhibition Architectures pour l'avenir at la villa
Noailles, Hyères*

*03 / Léa Peckre x Maison Lejaby, 2014.
Art Direction for the identity capsule
collection of Léa Peckre for Maison
Lejaby. Photo by Harley Weir. Styling by
Lotta Volkova. Modelled by Marianne
Fassarella Da Silva (Wome).*

03

Violaine & Jérémy

Art direction, graphics, illustration
Paris

Violaine & Jérémy is Violaine Orsoni and Jérémy Schneider whose superb design sense and skills can be attested by their graphic identities, pattern design and editorial design created for fashion brands such as Dior and FrenchTrotters, publications (Influencia, Le Food), cultural institution as the National Orchestra of Lorraine and music label. Their intricate surrealist hand illustrations as a subtle nod to vintage-style portraitures distinguish their work. The duo also dabbles in typography where appropriate.

01 / *Théâtre des Bouffes du Nord Iden-tity, 2015. Art direction, graphic design and typography for Parisian institution Le Théâtre des Bouffes du Nord.*

01

Can you tell us something about your creations?

We like to think of our graphic design as seductive, elegant, meticulous and timeless. Our illustration is subtle, ironic, technic and beautiful.

How would you identify your artistic style with French culture?

It influences our work a lot because we always try to pursue the timeless aesthetic. We've got historical references that have travelled through time and haven't aged. Our inspiration mainly comes from the part of French history that spans from current times to all the way back to the days of Louis XIV, as well as French and European philosophical concepts by the likes of Michel Foucault, Gilles Deleuze, Friedrich Nietzsche and Arthur Schopenhauer. We like adding a modern twist to the timelessness in our work. This twist, comes mostly from our irony and offbeat humour, is our way of showing our perspective.

How do you usually get yourself ready to create?

Inspiration works like a virtuous circle. First, input always comes naturally from something we like or we're passionate with. Then we do research about it. And these researches nourish our inspiration. We exchange a lot of ideas with each other.

What makes you stay in France?

We don't know. Maybe because nothing feels like home and maybe because our French way of life is deeply rooted in us.

Where can you find inspiring influences in France?

Absolutely everywhere. First of all, History. Then philosophy, food, paintings, sculpture, architecture and music. Basically, everything about France is inspiring.

How would you define French creativity?

For us, the best of French creativity mostly resides in our ideas, intellectual and philosophical debates and invention of a unique social organisation. Liberté, Égalité, Fraternité.

What kind of creative practice would you consider unorthodox in the country ?

There's no solid conclusion about unorthodox practice, but food here is definitely creative. It's incredible to see the chefs at work. It's a kind of pleasure that never gets old.

What do you plan to do next?

We are designing scarves for a fashion label and working on the identity of a super nice exhibition about contemporary arts and crafts at Le Musée des Arts Décoratifs in Paris. Other than that, we plan to live a long life exploring happiness in every possible way.

02

02 / *Welcome to the Jungle, 2015.
Art direction, editorial design and
typography for a quarterly thematic
employment guide. Cover by Priscille
Depinay. Illustrations by Julia Lamou-
reux, Emmanuel Espinasse, Charlotte
Pollet, Laura Ancona, Priscille Depinay.*

*03 / Emmanuelle, 2012. Graphic
identity and illustration for a
crew of filmmakers, Emmanuelle.
Photo by Olivia Fremineau.*

*04 / Popote's, 2014. Graphic
identity for a group of French-
born caterer in New York. Photo
by Olivia Fremineau.*

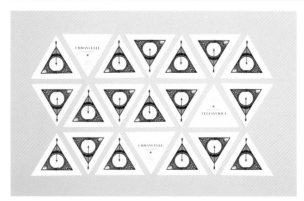

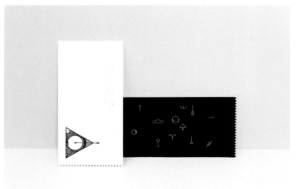

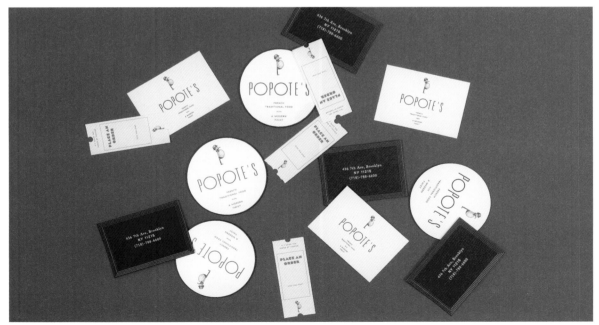

Virginie
Morgand

Illustration
Paris

Inspired by hands-on printing techniques and the children's books and toys she collects, Virginie Morgand creates vibrant images marked by hand-drawn shapes and bright colours. Virginie has a background in animation but her knowledge in screenprinting refashioned her visual language into chipper, organic graphics often packed with energy. Her recent projects have been produced for Martigues music and dance festival, children's books publishers (MeMo and Wide Eyed Editions), and The Sunday Times, etc. Portrait ©L'instant Parisien.

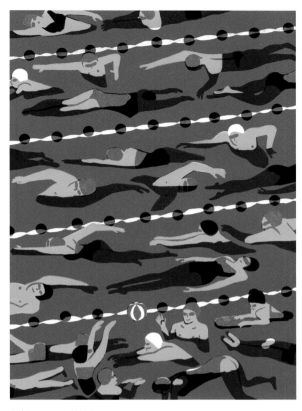

01 / Crowd series, 2014. Tricolour screenprint posters explore pattern compositions and colour interactions for Slow Galerie, Paris.

01

Can you tell us something about your creations?

I love bright colours. I often use primary colours as a base, and then I get more colours by superimposing the primary ones with a certain density. I always try to work with a limited range of colours. I illustrate for brands, festivals and create advertising posters. I also do editorial illustrations for magazines and children's books. I like working on personal projects such as screenprint posters when I take a break.

How would you identify your artistic style with French culture?

I think I'm in a 'family' of illustrators close to Mid-century art, somewhere between graphic design and illustration.

How do you usually get yourself ready to create?

When I have an illustration to complete, I think first about composition and colour. I make quick sketches with a pencil or pen, then do colour tests with markers on top. Occasionally I cut and assemble semi-transparent colour paper to create compositions and interesting colours. I redraw the draft I like most in Photoshop. When I screenprint posters, I often experiment on paper lying around me. Sometimes I integrate printing defects to create charming illustrations on computer.

What makes you stay in France?

France is a multicultural country with a long history. There are lots of different landscapes. I am inspired by Paris and also like the French coast with beautiful retro beaches as well as the south.

Where can you find inspiring influences in France?

I collect children's books, posters and toys from 1920s to 1960s and I am very sensitive to the printmaking techniques of yesteryear. Print defects bring a special charm to the image. I am also inspired by French artists such as Henri Matisse, Hervé Morvan, Bernard Villemot, René Gruau and other multidisciplinary European artists like Bruno Munari, Fredun Shapur and Olle Eksell.

How would you define French creativity?

Lots of French illustrators that inspire me have a playful and joyful approach to advertising, with simple shapes and a strong ideas.

What kind of creative practice would you consider unorthodox in the country?

Collective artists. Illustrators, graphic designers and typographers love working together in recent years to create beautiful handmade books, fanzines with experimental printing process. Some organise 'editions fairs' where you can meet the collectives and always discover something rich and different. I'm also very impressed by lots of French cartoonist for their satirical work in the press.

What do you plan to do next?

I love using handmade printing techniques. I would like to experiment with them on fabrics and wood when I have the time, and maybe I would create some patterns too.

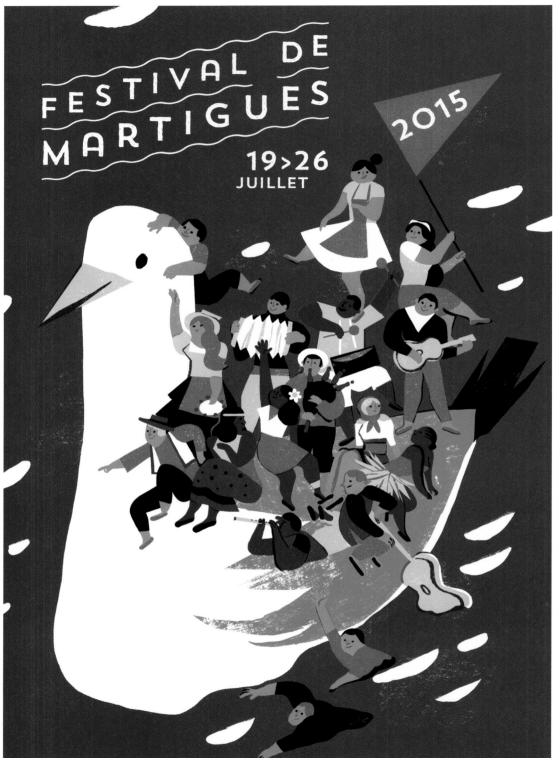

02 / Festival de Martigues posters, 2014-15. New brand identity
adds energy and a multicultural
feeling to the cultural festival.

02

FESTIVAL DE
MARTIGUES
20>28
JUILLET
2014

03 / *La Piscine, 2015. Screen-print posters for a solo exhibition at O!Galeria, Porto, in 2015.*

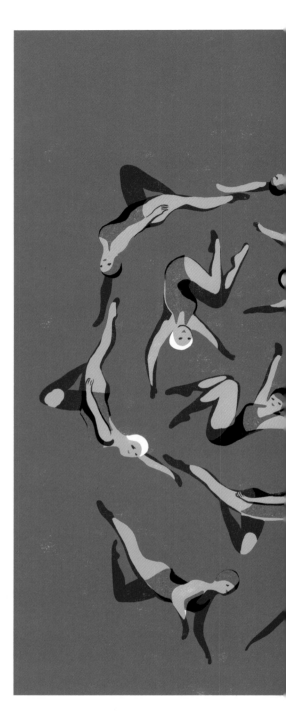

Index